ART NOUVEAU G

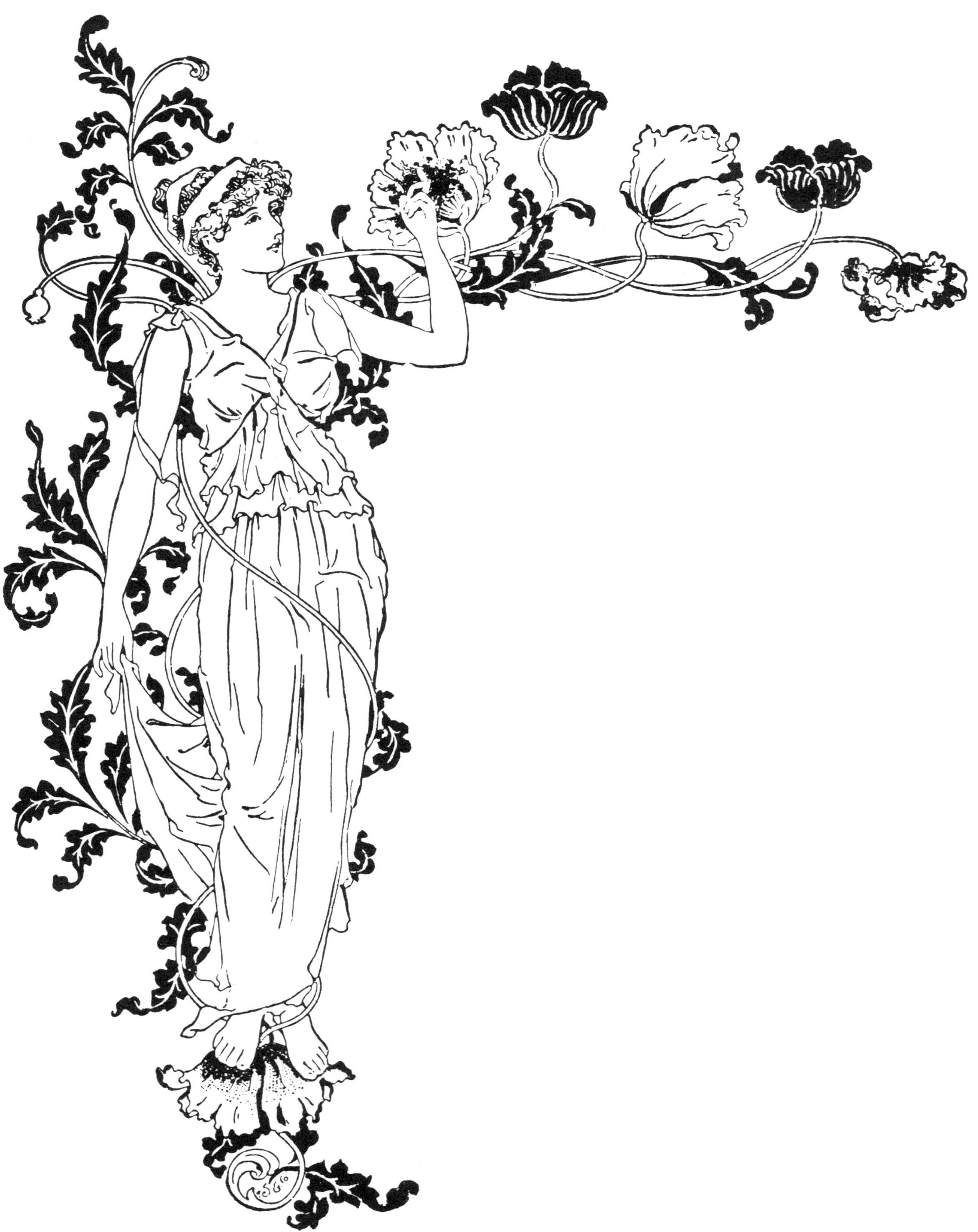

OTTO LORENZ

# ART NOUVEAU
## GRAPHIC ART

PADRE PUBLISHERS

Translated by Otto Lorenz

PADRE PUBLISHERS


English Language Rights, Padre Publishers
8195 Ronson Road, San Diego, CA 92111 U.S.A.
Fax (619) 277-5790

Printed in the U.S.A.

ISBN 1-57133-444-0

# CONTENTS

The particular of the epoch and its style is in the spiritual attitude, in the vital consciousness which is taking shape in all media: in Richard Strauss's music as well as in the poems by Rainer Maria Rilke, in Segantini's paintings and in Beardsley's drawings, in Toulouse-Lautrec's posters and in Gallé's glass vases, in Gallimard's Métro entrances, in van de Velde's chairs and Leistikov's wallpaper. Every one of these artistic media is equally accessible to the style, each of them expresses one common thing: the desire to create a counterbalance to the soulless mechanization and industrialization which began to take over the whole world from the middle of the 19th century onwards. They did not want to stop this development, on the contrary, they wanted to make use of the many possibilities; but they also wanted to prevent that, with the requirements of industrial manufacture, the compulsion for rationalization and therefore also to a nationalization of the products, the consumer for whom all these things had been manufactured would be forgotten: man.

Hans H. Hofstätter

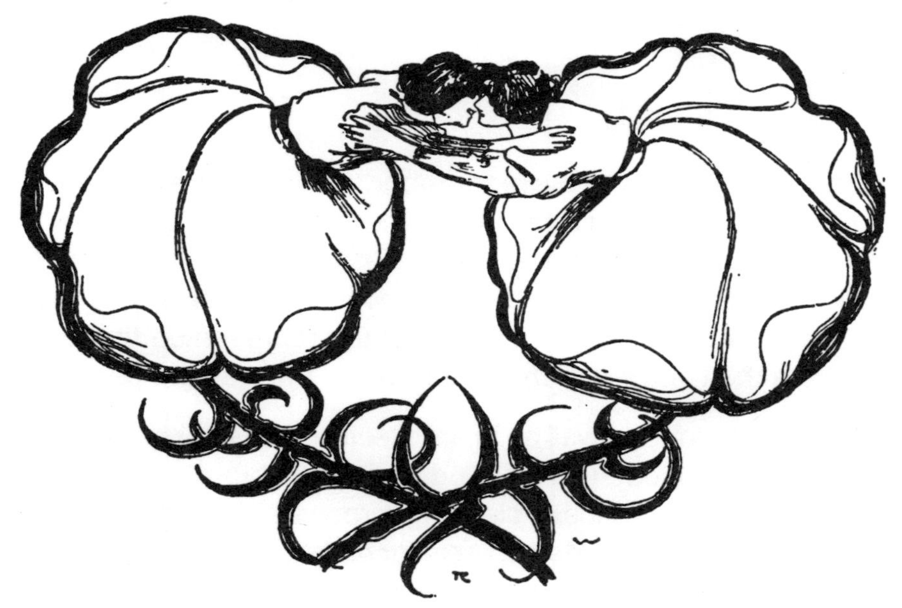

# Introduction

Art Nouveau was an artistic movement which began around the middle of the 19th century and had a style forming influence on all areas of artistic life till approximately 1910.

The naming and ascribing of individual works varied. In England it was originally called *Modern Style*, in France, where they wished to express the fact that the new art came from English cultural circles, *Style Moderne.* In Holland the movement was called *Nieuwe Kunst* until the term *L'Art Nouveau* became accepted everywhere outside Germany where the style retained the name *Jugendstil*. The Name *Art Nouveau* had its origins in the name of an art gallery close to the legendary *Passage de l'Opera* which was opened in 1895 by the Hamburg-born Siegfried Bing. The opening of the gallery was proclaimed by a very effective poster of the new style, designed by Felix Vallotton. The term which had been adopted in Germany, *Jugendstil*, took its name from the title of the review *Jugend* which had dedicated itself to this style.

The term Art Nouveau was at first just used in the area of applied art, in painting it can only be recognized looking back historically and then only hesitantly.

The characteristic elements of Art Nouveau are the emphasis on ornamentation, the strong stylization with rhythmic exaggeration of the form and the dominance of line. In this context, the clear relationship to Gothic art has often been mentioned. In fact there are a great many parallels between the two styles, in basic idea as well as in decoration. It should be remembered, of course, that the artists of the 19th and 20th centuries were very aware of the art and intellectual historical assessments of Gothic art and its characteristic style.

The climbing ornamental plant is the most important decorative element in the new art. The long female figures in flowing robes, dancers or standing figures beside extremely elegant animals such as swans or cranes are expression of style and time. The representation of realistic workers, for example, which was matter-of-course for the Expressionists, is unknown in Art Nouveau. At the most the represented figures are occupied with a task. But here the task is not important, rather the way the person looks.

In the area of arts-and-crafts as well as in architecture and interior design the new style was introduced with a consciousness of good craftsmanship so that often an especially good symbiosis of a new, aesthetically pleasing form was created with functionality and suitable use of material. Well designed objects for daily use ranked high in people's lives up to the 1920s. *Functionality and material logic* were the main dictates for the Art Nouveau designers. Art Nouveau was an attempt to create a common mandatory canon of form which was to become a new spirit seeking lifestyle without the stylistic weight and outer expression of previous developments in art.

At first the style was an expression of a new mental attitude. *Sincerity* was the basis of this new way of thinking. The magazine *Jugend* was sub-titled *Wochenschrift für Kultur und Leben* (Weekly review for culture and life), and this reflected the fact that the thoughts and wishes of all the artists and authors were focused in all directions. Followers of the movement wished to have a reforming influence on all areas of life and intellect. Emanating from the weltanschauung, the various applied arts, literature, dance, theatre as well as the crafts, architecture, book design, cultivated living and design of objects for everyday use were seen as a general synopsis.

Admittedly the demand for a total effect was a basis for the downfall of the movement. The power was not strong enough for a complete reform of life on all levels. What the spiritual leaders in literature, art und crafts created were objects which, because of their unconditional quality, could only be made for an elite minority. Only a small, rich circle could afford books from *Insel*, glasses from *Gallé*, interiors from *Peter Behrens*. However, industrial mass production avidly grabbed at Art Nouveau ornamentation which for a short time gave a false impression of good design in an industrial world which lacked quality. An ornamental epidemic began. Within a few decades Art Nouveau inundated people's lives so much that the willingness to accept it was exhausted, especially as it was used in increasingly senseless ways. Eventually a critic wrote, "You can't go out in the street anymore without bumping your head against the spiral ornament of an Art Nouveau candelabrum." The surrogates from the anonymous industrial manufacture led the style ad absurdum and ruined it with overpowering decoration.

In a satirical article by Gumppenberg in the review *Jugend* (which will be reported on later in more detail), the increase in the production of sham was heavily criticized, "Recently the *Jugend* came to the dear God in Heaven with such a long face. The Lord never hated that type of person and accepted it quite well and asked how it was getting on, how many subscribers it had, whether it had been imprisoned and so on and finally why it was so angry — Dear God, said the Jugend, my good reputation is being destroyed! Or rather it is being misused. The people on Earth are making the most outrageous objects from plaster, tin, glass, paper, cardboard, leather, zinc and whatever you like and more or less put them on my bill. They call every pot which has a hideous stylized lily or a female with a ridiculous hairstyle or an orchid *Jugendstil*. They call it *Jugendstil* when any cigarette packet or casket or a photograph frame has a grotesque figure pressed, stuck or painted onto it, which is half human or half ornament and as distorted as possible. Every wallpaper, every tie material, every cotton cloth whose pattern is half hideous, half Japanese, is *Jugendstil*. The chairs on which you cannot sit, the cupboards in which you cannot put anything, glasses which you cannot drink from, spoons which you cannot eat from are all called *Jugendstil*! It's enough to drive you mad. Surely I don't just imagine that I discovered the new style: I have only nurtured and promoted it with my modest means. And now I should bear the cost for all the misunderstandings and abuse, for all the corruption by crude mass production industry which only produces *Jugendstil* because Rococo patterns do not sell. The fellows overlook the fact that I have brought to light a wealth of good and beautiful things for which I gladly accept the term *Jugendstil*. I am fed up! I have had enough! I am getting out of it — I will have myself renamed."

Even Friedrich Ahlers-Hestermann began his work of fundamental importance, *Stilwende*, which appeared in 1941 and was meant to draw the general public's attention to the basics of Art Nouveau, with the word "The vision which we have when we hear the term Art Nouveau is ludicrous and hideous: plant type worms entwine remodelled sofas, impossible masses of hair from concavely pressed woman's heads form an ashtray, and several waterlilies have succeeded in moving onto coloured tiled stoves." In another part of the book he writes about the spread of Art Nouveau, "It was as lovely as a famous play how the flood rolled up in large lines, whose crashing impact crushed the decay, the outmoded and indolent. When it ebbed and flowed back sparkling, it left on the beach algae, jellyfish and foul smelling seaweed: those are the rests which we have today. Only a few know the world which is not dissimilar to that in the crystal depths of the ocean which they belong to from a distance, as misunderstood, cheapened industrialized travesties of courageous artistic thoughts."

Forty years later, these dreadful visions are gone. Young people today see Art Nouveau as a discovery. And time shows that the dominance of the style has an effect on the future. The Art Nouveau movement became a main inspiration for modern art. In the Art Nouveau years are the beginnings of all tendencies to spiritual awakening which give people in the 20th century hope for inner development.

Peter Behrens wrote, "Now we have an indication that the new style will come, not emanating from the old which is partly there already, at least in the beginning. Certainly we will have to keep our eyes open and have a cheerful desire and belief in the beautiful, then we will recognize that something is happening which corresponds more deeply to our life than those sought after, bizarre forms which appear 'modern' on the surface but are mostly just loose commodities from people who quickly make novelty a way of earning money. What is coming has an inner effect and is neither randomly invented nor playfully put together from the established forms."

The Art Nouveau era was also the beginning of what has been described as *exhibition art*. The democratization of art made the artist an economic factor. Traditional ties of artists to a patron from the ruling classes gradually disappeared (artists were increasingly only sponsored from above). The ties to the Church as a client had been broken earlier. Art had to seek a market.

Also successful artists whose abilities and connections had helped them to a public (and paid) office had to distinguish themselves just to keep their posts, all others needed the establishment of a public to achieve fame and with this a livelihood.

This making of a public came about, on the one hand, through officially organized exhibitions such as the *World Exhibition* where the applied arts and the arts and crafts were well represented. It also was formed by unions of like-minded artists who organized their *Salons* and so created a mouthpiece to a wide section of the public.

Besides this there were also various reviews and magazines, and last but not least the private initiatives of friends of the arts who were also merchants and businessmen who helped artists to achieve fame by exhibiting their works in their galleries.

"This *exhibition art*, as it was already called around 1900, resulted from an institutionalized dialogue between producers and consumers: beside such a state of affairs, exhibitions also enabled an emotional relationship between 'exhibitionist' art and 'voyeurist' observer (because on the one hand they did not force to buy and on the other hand there was an accumulation of many individual objects for sale)." (Simon)

Apart from the magazines which were especially close to Art Nouveau such as *Pan*, *Jugend*, *Insel*, *Simplizissimus* and *Ver Sacrum*, which will be dealt with in the chapter about the importance of graphic printing, there were a great deal of reviews in Germany which dealt with Art Nouveau in comprehensive articles — admittedly also critical in part.

A wider circle of readers interested in interior design and questions of good taste were, above all, catered for in magazines and reviews such as *Dekorative Kunst*, *Deutsche Kunst und Dekoration* and *Die Kunst für Alle.* Politically orientated magazines such as *Die Zukunft*, *Die Zeit*, *Die Gegenwart* or *Die neue Rundschau* dealt less with artistic themes, but when they did, their opinions were respected. And finally there was also a series of — widely distributed — reviews such as *Der Kunstwart* which was read in conservative circles and which tended more towards folk art (sometimes also to "national" art). They only very occasionally advertised Art Nouveau artists or parts of their work. But on the whole it can be said that the magazines had a considerable influence on the spread of the new art.

# Sources of Art Nouveau

Official painting in the 19th century, such as was cultivated and taught in the academies and was generally bound to a bourgeois lifestyle, mainly had a historical content, based on the technical virtuosity of the Old Masters. Artists of that time honoured the classical return to picture themes and forms from antiquity and the Renaissance. This art gradually ossified in an increasingly empty, barely creative mannerism. The large scale paintings showed antique or early German pomposity in a theatrical-realistic fashion. In Germany the main representatives were Karl von Piloty, Wilhelm von Kaulbach and Anton von Werner. Peaks, such as the bombastic, spectacular shows from Hans Makart, which made improvement impossible in terms of composition and talent, confined themselves to the decorative representation of historical events without any development in thought or demand for artistic liveliness. Although there are suggestions in the execution of Makart's paintings which show the beginnings of something new, it was left to his pupils such as Gustav Klimt to make this new era obvious.

How overrated this official painting was is shown by the fact that from the French artists of the Second Republic, who were honoured and given well paid official commissions, not one retained any meaning for the future.

Economically, the so-called *period of promoterism*, the time after 1850, was an epoch of progress and unlimited capitalism. A complete section of the public, mainly people from petit bourgeois families succeeded by means of commercial farsightedness and heedless speculation in achieving a great deal of money in a relatively short time. Capital and profit took the place of family background and true merit. The amassing of fortune became an end in itself. "Money became a symbol of happiness and an object to be hunted as never before, and an invention such as the telegraph served primarily to increase the international stocks and shares market. Wealth and care are the poles of bourgeois life." (Ahlers-Hestermann)

It is, of course, obvious that the greedy amassing of money could only be gained from the backs of enslaved industrial workers. It was also clear, at least in the people's subconscious, that an enormous social crisis was approaching. However, instead of facing it in spirit and therefore developing qualities of leadership corresponding to the influence, the upper middle class withdrew into a pompous illusory world.

The upstarts' attempts to achieve prestige corresponding to their new status was made easier by the government through purchasable titles and honours which could only be obtained for a lot of money. "Wealth wants to show itself, especially when it is new. The rooms were filled, the contours of the sofas and chairs were curved and all sorts of adornments were stuck on." (Ahlers-Hestermann) Personal lack of style was best concealed by a recourse to traditional styles from the past. Illustrative for the spirit of the age was the lack of culture in living standards in these circles. The rooms, crammed with any style of furniture, were mere status symbols and only suitable for satisfying a vain social prestige.

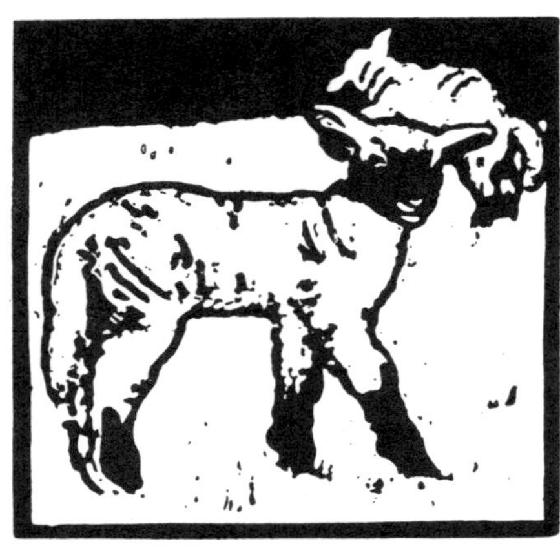

An especially awful staffage were rooms in the *studio style*. Artists' studios at that time were packed full with all imaginable knick-knacks which could possibly serve their painting. They looked more like property rooms in a theatre than places of creative action. The same awful chambers enriched with a bulging divan in a cozy corner were for the people a symbol of a slightly crazy artistic life and therefore worth imitating. "Modern" interior designers on the other hand campaigned for furnishings in certain styles: for example Gothic or Moresque or Renaissance imitation. In 1876 in Munich the German Renaissance was declared to be the national style, "Only when the applied arts are established in every home, will they be able to fully pursue their refining influence on the country."

The style of painting which was demanded by the governing bodies corresponded to all this. While the great art of the time — Leibl, Thoma, Feuerbach — modestly flourished, relegated to the background, a large flood poured into the average German house from the historical painting: the splendour of the costumes and the glittering embellishments were in contrast to "the prose of everyday life", in other words, the work of earning money.

In order that the course of art would not change and that it further served patriotism and glorification of the ruling dynasty, only party line artists were placed in positions of importance in the academies by the ruling bodies. It happened occasionally that the politicians interfered when it seemed to them that there was a chance of an unwelcome change in the teaching posts. William II declared, "An art form which deviates from the laws and borders which I have drawn up is no longer art, it is factory work, trade, and art is not allowed to become either of those. With the often misused word 'freedom' and using this as an excuse people often decline into boundlessness, unrestraint and self-conceit."

In all countries there was a relatively early movement by mainly young artists to detach themselves from the official art world and to create something new. Even the Romantic

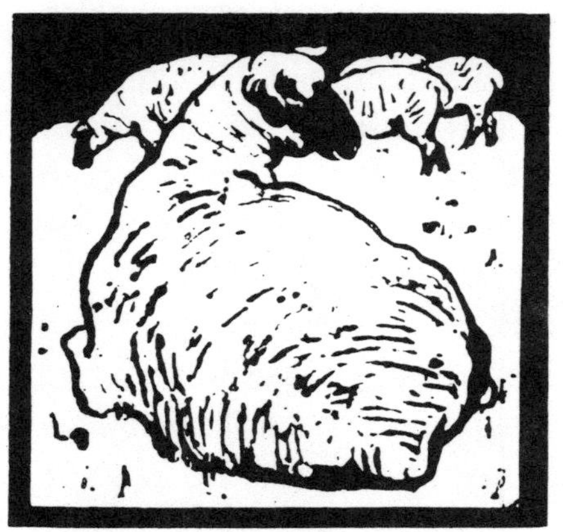

artists had restless ideas of freedom and development in art as well as in life, and in their painting they realized the effects of a new spirit of the age which was surging in the consciousness of open-minded people. Revolutionary ideas were adopted in a new art form. Caspar David Friedrich had brought a wealth of world-changing thoughts into his paintings which, if he had spoken them aloud, would have brought him into serious political difficulties.

The intellectual elite of the age were activated by the pictures of the Romantics and were searching for the realization of a different lifestyle.

Groups such as the Nazarenes, who formed a spiritual union in 1809 and with their oppositional ideas deliberately opposed the academical style of painting, also formed a strict codex for their way of living which was far removed from a middle class lifestyle. They moved to the monastery Sant' Isidoro in Rome and in a monastical brotherhood attempted to "live a holy art". They dressed themselves like Dürer's self-portrait with uncut hair, parted in the middle, and long beards and clothed themselves in flowing robes (in the Italian vernacular "alla Nazareno"). Living in such a way, they attempted "a renewal of art based on the spirit of the Old Masters".

Admittedly, most of their themes were quite common — above all Christian Church painting — and they only detached themselves from accepted styles of painting in their landscapes.

The English Pre-Raphaelites tended still more to a lifestyle with newly created standards. They introduced occultist secret society rules into their *Pre-Raphaelite Brotherhood*. The leading member of this group was Dante Gabriel Rosetti who built his work on the compositions filled with rhythmic movement by William Blake. Apart from him the inspired John Everett Millais made interesting artistic discoveries which look as if they were painted in the 20th century. The Pre-Raphaelites took on the challenges of the Nazarenes for simplicity and ethical seriousness in art without placing the religious element in the forefront.

Rosetti mostly painted from literary themes. Dante or the search for the Holy Grail are his main themes. He was able to create a connection between literature and his painting. The female figure is always present in his paintings. As Pandora, Sibylle, Venus or Astarte "she is always a complete woman, powerful and at the same time affectionate. Often she seems fateful, in the same painting also sometimes, facing another figure which she seems to mirror. Intensive colours and decorative elements give her an enigmatic aura somewhere between dream and reality". (Philippe Robert-Jones) It is clear that the elements which would later distinguish the works of the symbolists were first obvious here. The ability of the group to realize their aims not only in painting but also in word and therefore to be able to publish the knowledge of use of line and space which they had gained continued with their pupils Edward Burre-Jones, William Morris and Walter Crane.

William Morris, schooled in the spirit of the Pre-Raphaelites, was also a politician and a convinced social reformer, however, in his chief artistic quality he was an artist-craftsman. Together with the Rosetti pupil Edward Burre-Jones he created the first typographically designed and illustrated books in the *Modern Style* apart from creating arts-and-crafts designs. Their works very quickly spread and had a lasting effect as they were based on an enormous reformatory engagement. Morris did not just advocate an improvement in the situation of the exploited factory workers, he also saw beyond the material needs the clear danger that without the intervention of forming artists in the rapidly spreading industrial production there would be a spiritual impoverishment of unimaginable dimensions. "The machine — a new standard for life's speed, which for thousands of years has been measured by the pace of a man or a horse, by the oar stroke or the wind in the sails — made industrial cities from fields. Its iron arm created colossal factories, but crushed craftsmanship and took the soul from form." (Ahlers-Westermann)

A technical development provided for a quick spread of the new artistically designed books. In 1811 F. König invented the high-speed printing machine. By 1850 it had reached a stage of technical development which enabled the manufacture of well printed books in large amounts. It was no longer just a small elite circle who could now afford books, the new illustrated books were increasingly bought by a large group of the population. It should not be forgotten that in those decades the majority of the western European population had left illiteracy behind and increasingly took part in the intellectual und political developments.

Morris's special interest was the typographical revival of the carefully designed book. In 1888 he created his own establishment for the creation of these, the Kelmscott Press. Book decoration and illustration made great progress in those years. The thematic circle of illustrated books was also swiftly extended. In this connection Walter Crane is to be thanked for a novelty in books: he made picture books for children and so created a completely new type of book. Apart from his work as painter and illustrator, he also wrote theoretical essays on design problems which were very effective.

In the work of these three personalities the intellectual and practical beginnings of Art Nouveau and at the same time a major part of the theoretical basis of the new art can be seen. The decorative seriousness with which it bound a loyalty to material with the new style in art-craft design and applied book graphics had a lasting effect on further developments. Complexity of arts, a union of art and living in which everyone should have a part was aimed for. It was firstly meant to serve an education in aesthetics and secondly a perfection in craftsmanship in all areas of life. Morris consequently realized these new ideals as far as the formation of socialist co-operatives in which furniture, material and tools were made in careful, skilled form and design. The firm Morris, Marshall & Faulkner became the basis of the arts-and-crafts movement.

In France, the young Impressionists were a similar source of reform and stimulus. Unmoved by the enmity from the general public and the ignorance of their academic colleagues, they blazed themselves a trail, far removed from traditional, classical painting. They discovered the autonomous power of pure colour as an element of design and accorded colour in its relationship to light and air the main place in their pictures with an absolute disregard of the picture theme which was traditionally the actual purpose of any artistic act before then. Impressionism ignored everything in content, contemplative painting, sentimentality or moralizing expression which had been successful with the public before, it declared the picture theme to be completely irrelevant. The external covering of things in shimmering light, the atmosphere, these were the things which they wished to represent. The realization of impressions became the purpose of painting. A group of painters — their spokesman was Seurat — decomposed their paintings, similar to modern four-colour printing, into individual particles of colour placed next to each other. This technique, which has entered art history as pointillism, was in theory correct from a physical point of view, but it was never able to completely satisfy in the composition. However, soon several of the Impressionists recognized that with their way of seeing things, the body of the objects had to be lost behind the colourfully shimmering areas, and that the picture which resulted showed a weak lack of structure. Therefore painters such as Renoir began again to sketch in their pictures with firmly established lines. It was Cézanne who first found a form which brought harmony between Impressionistic colour effects and composition. Van Gogh and many other young artists learned from him. A change took place within a section of the Impressionist movement and this group of artists was receptive for the knowledge which drifted to them from Art Nouveau.

Western artists received further stimulus from a completely different cultural development: A strong cultural impulse came to Europe from the Far East, especially China. This had occured once before in the Rococo period. In those days fine artistic painting and crafts had taken the houses of the ruling classes by storm. Expensive porcelain, silk wallpaper, lacquer from the Middle Kingdom became dominating decorative requisites in the Rococo residences. The Far East remained a decorative element in the bourgeois design world of the 19th century. However, the Japanese coloured woodcuts from Hokusai, Hiroshige and Utamaro which were first shown at the Paris World Exhibition in

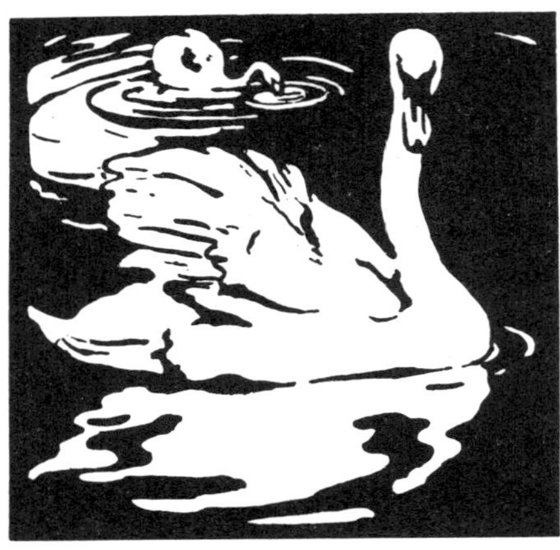

1867 were a sensation. In Japan, the woodcuts from the Ukiyo-e-style were regarded as folk art and were paid relatively little attention. They were definitely not regarded as a higher art form. However, for Western art the works were like a beacon. After the forceful opening of Japanese ports by American warships in 1853, this country, which had until then been shut away from the world, rapidly orientated itself politically, economically and culturally towards the West. From then on Japan took part in the World Exhibitions and, as well as porcelain and crafts, brought a great many woodcuts onto the Western market in the 18th century. The brilliant use of area without modelling shadows or perspective depths, the elegant flow of the line and the consequently simplified composition fascinated the young group of seeking artists in Paris. The enormous colourfulness, a printing quality which was unknown in the West and last but not least the incredible freedom in choice of theme were reasons why they were so attracted to the woodcuts. The design principles of Japanese woodcut art were clearly understandable so that many artists were able to include perceptions from Eastern art as a liberating element in their new works. Without the intervention of Japanese woodcuts in Western art the formation of Art Nouveau would most certainly have been different, would have taken a poorer and more rigid course.

Siegfried Bing whose gallery in Paris had given art Nouveau its name had had a shop in Paris since 1871 in which he sold crafts imported from Japan, especially woodcuts. He also edited a magazine called *Le Japon Artistique* which incidentally was published in Leipzig in Germany with the title *Japanischer Formenschatz*. Bing also introduced another novelty to the Parisian art scene: he was one of the first who got to know the work of Louis Tiffany and the new line of American Art Nouveau graphics and introduced them to Paris.

Another movement in applied arts which developed from the rejection of the official history painting and led to Art Nouveau was Symbolism. The Symbolists sought their themes in areas which played either no part or at the most a secondary role on the surface of human life. Symbolism was the visual expression of a literary and intellectual

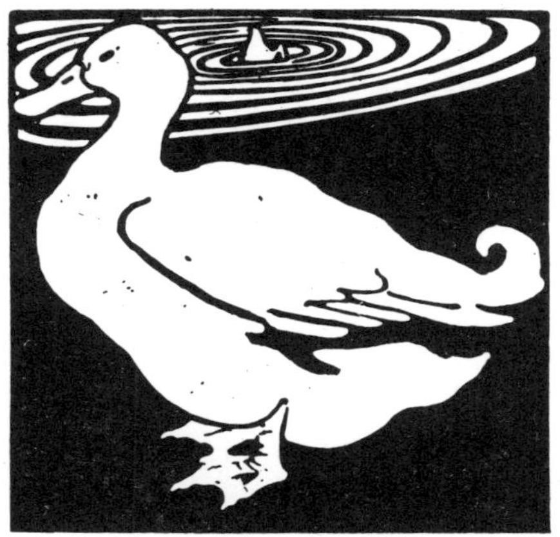

movement from very different influences. Its themes were based on dreams, magic, sleep, fantasy, death and afterlife. Hallucinations and visionary mysticism were sources of this art in which the spirit had absolute precedence over matter. Contrary to Impressionism, which was a purely artistic movement, Symbolism developed from thoughts and dreams. Discussion was the root of this art. From the discussion, followers of the movement wrote poetry or painted, and — at least in France — the close contact of the painters and poets of this style was very stimulating.

The official art of the era was only an ostentatious mirror image of a hard materialism which ruled civilization. Poets such as Verlaine, Rimbaud, Maeterlinck and Verhaeren rebelled against this. Painters such as Moreau, Redon and Puvis de Chavannes followed them and gave their vision a picture form. They opposed the economic and technical trends and accorded the spiritual priority over matter. They mobilized all the powers which consciousness was endowed with: Imagination instead of inspiration was their weltanschauung. "Courbet's realism and the landscape painters of his school — including Monet's Impressionism — dispensed with fantasy and made the representation of reality their only aim. In the full light of the one as in the semi-dark of the other, the subjectivity was missing, no matter how sensitive Sisley and Pissarro are or how broad-minded Monet's visions are or how passionate Manet is." (Jean Cassou)

A basis for the Symbolist poets and writers were Charles Baudelaire and Stephan Mallarmé. From Germany, Friedrich Nietzsche was a spiritual foundation. From him emanates the thought that a work of art exists to refresh the desires of man on his long path towards death by conveying a little intoxication and madness.

Goya, Blake, Füssli and Turner were predecessors of Symbolism and also sources for the Nazarenes and Pre-Raphaelites. Turner, in his attempts to represent atmosphere, was a predecessor of Impressionism and also a pioneer of Symbolism. It was not just the effect of light which occupied him, but he also introduced imaginary ingredients into his work. His last paintings completely dispensed with reality in favour of fantastic visions.

Füssli's works were strongly in the grip of the expression of inner tension and erotic dreams. Blake, on the other hand, was a visionary. In his work, he attempted to create a connection between the eternal and the temporal. He gave earthly form to perceptions from supernatural worlds in his paintings. Goya eventually escaped the horrors of war and withdrew to the world of his own obsessive ideas. All four were the basis on which the Symbolists built. We see their work again everywhere as a starting point for those Art Nouveau painters who are dedicated to Symbolism.

Two phenomena distinguish the development of Art Nouveau from other modern movements in art. Firstly the explosive speed with which the style entered the consciousness of many artists and, above all, the general public, is incredible. Secondly, Art Nouveau was always very closely connected to the applied arts, especially to the crafts.

When one considers the long struggle the artists of Impressionism and Expressionism had until their work was no longer ridiculed and rejected, it is astounding to see how the Art Nouveau movement was commonly accepted in everyday life within a few years.

There is a close connection between the many possibilities of using the style and its spread: The field of arts and crafts was especially receptive to new forms. The first World Exhibition, which was opened in Hyde Park by Queen Victoria in 1851, was meant to demonstrate progress in all fields and so show the glory of the British Empire. However, it showed an unprecedented qualitative decline in the craft exhibits. Lumbersome forms and workmanship which was not longer suited to the materials used were evident. A new spirit had to come which would again bring form and ability to bear. Because of this, the path was smoothed for a willing acceptance of the new style. The beginning change to industrial manufacture and the mass production which went along with this also served to spark off the search for something new in the skilled trades.

Because of the positive acceptance which Art Nouveau found in all circles of the population, new contracts which arose were preferably commissioned and carried out in the new style. Thus the classical example of this can be seen in the building of the first underground in 1900 in Paris: the new entrances to the Métro stations were designed by the architect Hector Guimard using the *Style Moderne*. In this way a millionfold public, i. e. the population of the metropolis, went past Art Nouveau objects in their day to day life. As opposed to the limitations of an artistic style which only found access in the fields of painting, graphics and sculpture, the penetration of Art Nouveau with its multifarious uses presented a complete pervasion of the public and private spheres of life.

The connections of the *performing arts* to Art Nouveau are manifold and varied. Later, the important factor of stage interpretation will be mentioned. Toulouse-Lautrec's oeuvre would not have been possible if it had not been for the world of cabaret and the many demimonde figures in Paris. The chanson singer Aristide Bruant with his Theatre Ambassadeurs live on in Lautrec's bold posters. Dancers such as Loïe Fuller with her metre wide flowing robes inspired artists from the whole of Europe: several artists, including Jules Chéret, Th. Th. Heine, Will Bradly and Koloman Moser honoured her with exciting graphical works. The actress Sarah Bernhardt became the upholder of a complete style in the pictures from Alfons Maria Mucha. Even the name May Belfort would be unknown to us if the works of Art Nouveau artists had not brought it a whiff of immortality — and she, with the interaction of her performance — had not influenced the artists' passions.

In the area of serious music, the operas were the main stimulus. In Beardsley's Wagner representations one cannot be sure if the wonderful series of graphics were inspired by Wagner as composer or as the creator of literary works. In the case of the *Wiener Werkstätten* it was clearly the music of Richard Strauss and Gustav Mahler which inspired the pictorial works with its magic.

However, the liveliest and most interactive contact existed between revue (poetry, song, dance and acting) and the visual artists in Munich and Berlin. Ernst von Wolzogen's *Überbrettl* which was established in 1901 in the Berlin Jugendstil building *Buntes Theater* (the name was inspired by Nietzsche's 'superman') was more literary orientated and its effect was limited. But in Munich *Die elf Scharfrichter* were settled in the middle of artistic life. The singer Marya Delvard became a "trademark" for revue, depicted by Th. Th. Heine in a skin-tight black dress. And in Kathi Kobus's artists' bar, in which *Simplizissimus* had settled, the list of players and regular guests is like an encyclopaedia of Jugendstil art and culture. "Heine, Gulbransson, Thöny, Reznicek, Wilke, Schulz gathered and quite often paid their bills with sketches which were a main attraction in the bar." (E. Pablé)

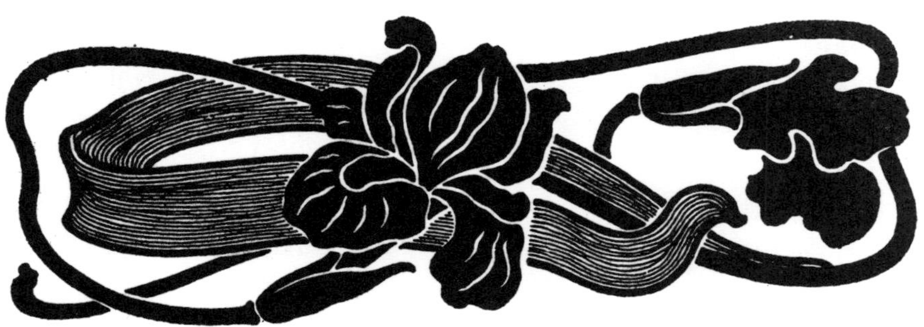

# History of Art Nouveau Graphic Art

Artists' consideration of the ideas of Art Nouveau and the conversion of the perceptions they gained into their work began at different times and with varying intensity in the European countries.

In France there was a movement of *inofficial art* which was very receptive to everything new. In Germany the new style was adopted much later than the analogous movement in the neighbouring Western countries. In England, however, the new style was based on arts-and-crafts considerations which had already been effective for decades there.

The already mentioned reform in the book manufacturing section with design and illustration which began around 1850 had consequences for another area — magazines. Here there was a wide field of expressive possibilities for a literary, illustrative-artistic criticism of contemporary issues. Graphic art was especially used as an essential decorative element by the publishers which meant ad hoc wide publicity for the respective artist.

An important magazine from that time was *The Yellow Book* and the artist who rapidly became famous with it was Aubrey Beardsley. He was an over-sensitive character who suffered from consumption in younger years and who died under the most awful conditions aged just twenty-six. He took refuge behind a dandy-like appearance which was meant to hide his weak constitution as well as his sensitive temperament. It was obvious that Beardsley shocked his fellow countrymen towards the end of an exceptionally prude Victorian era. But there were also circles who admired him for his perversity and decadent spirit and the impact of his eccentric works was certainly able to register a certain spectacular success.

His unparalleled talent and the stylistic perfection with which he began his work are of a greatness which make him unique. From the first day of his appearance on the art stage — and he most certainly saw art as a theatre — he was perfect, without being able to improve on his work, but also without weak points. He learned his expert handling of area and line from the Japanese, but with his precise coldness he fully outshined them. His work was an antithesis, difficult to understand. Biting satire, frigid eroticism, a cool, nervous, unbelievably exact line is the one side of his work, enchanting line movement, an almost morbid leaning to coquettish costumes, ecstatic enthusiasm for romantic-symbolistic picture content was the other side. He was a co-founder of *The Yellow Book*, and it existed from his graphic ideas. However, the magazine had to go out of publication for financial reasons. It was succeeded by *The Savoy*. The publisher of this was a successful London antiquarian who specialized in erotica.

Another artistic magazine from England was very important for the spread of the new style — also important beyond England's borders, as this review was also well received on the continent and became an inspiration for other magazines. *The Studio* had appeared in London since 1893. The activities of this institution were not just limited to tips and critical comments on the revolutionary artistic endeavours, it also showed path-breaking pictorial examples.

Apart from the high-speed printing press a further technical device was of great importance for Art Nouveau graphic art. Lithography which had been invented in 1799 by Aloys Senefelder was so technically perfected in England in the following decades that large coloured prints became possible. Although the machines and technical knowledge had been developed in England, leading artists in the country at first kept away from the new technique and the wonderful possibilities it offered. However, in France the new coloured printing methods fell on fertile ground. The painter Jules Chéret had learned the art of lithography in England and created the first coloured revue posters. Toulouse-Lautrec also adopted the new printing technique immediately and began by printing a very bold poster for the Moulin Rouge. The loose technique suited his graphic conceptions and the boldness of his lines eminently. Encouraged by Lautrec's amazing success Chéret now used his whole well-founded lithographic abilities. There was a sort of poster rivalry from which the whole of Paris profited.

In order to understand the public's excitement for the new posters, it has to be remembered that in the 1890s coloured pictures did not exist in the dismal grey streets. The people only knew single coloured written posters and the term advertising was still in its infancy. Then suddenly such an eruption of colour, verve and gay frivolity. The need for advertising space came just at the right time for Ernst Litfaß from Berlin with the erection of the advertising pillars which were named after him. Now in every large city, the colourful posters could be seen in the middle of the boulevard. It is understandable that Art Nouveau graphic art became famous overnight. Paris fell into a poster frenzy for years. There was almost no branch of the performing arts which did not invite a visit by means of poster: theatres, music-halls, concert halls, dance halls and ice rinks. But soon all sorts of articles were praised on posters. And soon art dealers and collectors realized the value of posters as works of art. Today in many collections of graphic art, posters can be found which have been carefully removed after use. However, many large reproduction businesses were established in those days. They offered an exclusive collector public freshly printed posters, often reduced in size solely for the purpose of collecting, quite often in versions without the printed advertising text.

A large number of artists dedicated themselves to the new art style. Toulouse-Lautrec and Chéret should be mentioned above all, they were joined by Théophile Alexandre Steinlen who was no less successful. He especially brought socio-critical components into the contents of his posters. While Chéret cultivated the brash elegance of his young girl figures in never-ending new variations, Lautrec sympathetically registered the ugliness in humans and his depraved environment, occasionally transfigured by a breath of warmth. Steinlen became the artist who uncovered and accused. Chéret's world is intact. Lautrec's world is sick. Steinlen fights for a better world.

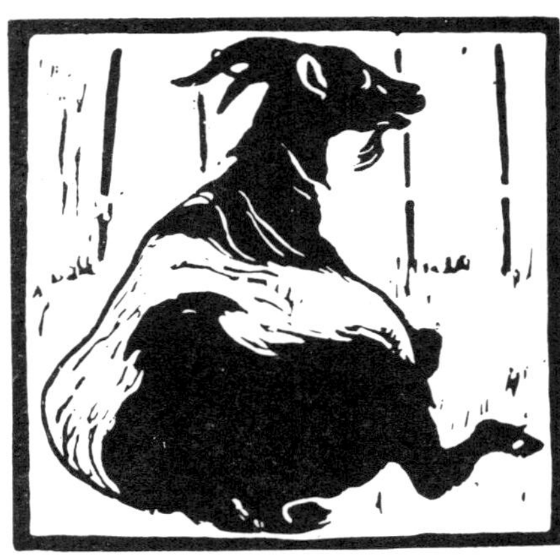

Jules Chéret brought the technique of colour lithography to the highest levels of perfection. He had learned the trade of lithographer, perfected his knowledge in England and, on his return to Paris, he opened his own lithographic workshop. It can be seen in his work that he drew his design on the stone himself. He thus raised lithography to an original artistic technique which was very well suited to the poster. His representations of elegant Parisian ladies, scantily dressed girls, dancers or café singers soon were given the name *Les Chérettes* by the public. These elegantly dressed, gracefully flowing female figures completely suited the Parisian taste of that time.

The works of the Swiss Eugène Grasset, who had lived in Paris since 1871, had a greater influence beyond the poster. Grasset was an architect and came to poster art by way of book design and applied art. His spiritual origins from the Pre-Raphaelites is very obvious. His art was a pattern for Bradley in America and for many artists in Germany.

A Czechoslovakian who lived in Paris was accorded a similar popularity to Chéret — Alfons Maria Mucha. His works carried the name *Style Mucha* in France and were often copied. Mucha's preferred theme in almost all his works was woman who he represented as an enigmatic dream figure. He was suddenly en vogue with a poster for the actress Sarah Bernhardt in the role of Gismonde. As a poster artist he was well occupied but also as a designer of jewelry. However, his reputation as a painter suffered somewhat due to his fame as a poster designer. This irritated him his life long as his main interest was painting.

The first artistic poster of quality which was successful appeared in England in 1871. It was Fred Walker's *The Woman in White*. It was already an Art Nouveau work. Aubrey Beardsley's works first appeared twenty years later, but then they rapidly awakened enthusiasm for the modern poster. In the same year, the first designs were created by the Brothers Beggarstoff, a pseudonym used by William Nicholson and James Pryde. The poster-like design of their works with abstracted contours and the simplest media was never achieved again.

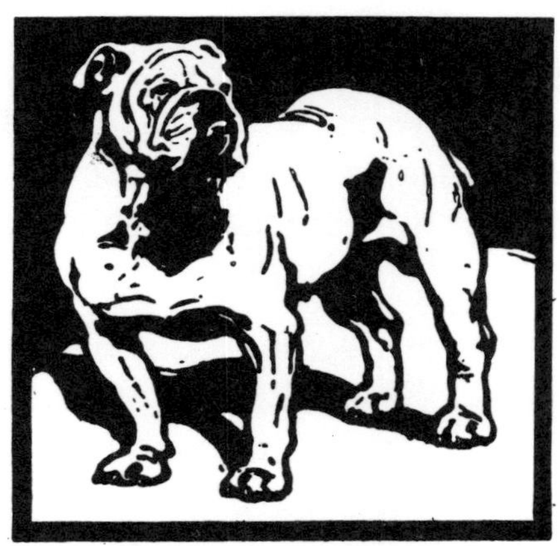

John Hassal und Dudley Hardy had the same role in England as Chéret in France, they became very versatile and received many commissions. Hardy became a master of the light hand. His posters for *A Gaiety Girl* in the Prince of Wales Theatre brought him world fame. They were reproduced in all magazines as especially good examples of posters from the London theatre scene.

France and England helped to bring poster art into being in America. Louis John Rhead got to know Grasset's works in Paris in 1894 and after his return he dedicated himself completely to poster art with which he achieved tremendous popularity within a few years. His posters were directive for the artistic poster in North America. The posters by William H. Bradley were equally successful. Bradley did not just work as a poster artist, he gained his true importance as a typographer, book designer and illustrator. His influences in European bibliographic art can be seen in this field. He created new standards with his journal *Bradley: His Book* for which he was editor, writer, artistic director, designer and printer.

Great developments had also been made in France in the last decades of the 19th century in the book and magazine ornamentation sectors. In England a small circle adhered to the new style and sought to realize the new spirit in their art, while in France a large number of artists tended towards Art Nouveau in the field of graphic art. Paul Gauguin had a key position in leading Impressionism to Art Nouveau. One journal was important for graphic art: *La Revue Blanche* with its artists Pierre Bonnard, Edouard Vuillard, Felix Vallotton and Henri de Toulouse-Lautrec. Henry van de Velde and the Norwegian Edvard Munch were also often to be seen in the editorial office.

From this group, the Swiss Felix Vallotton who lived in Paris was of overriding importance for Art Nouveau graphic art in France. No one had used the graphic effect of black and white areas as consequently as he where the insertion of both components always signalled opposites in content. His woodcuts with their cool two-dimensional areas and the hard contrasts between black and white brought him such rapid fame that people almost forgot that he was actually a painter who saw his main task in oil painting. When Vallotton felt that he had completed the black-and-white experiment, he consequently stopped and returned to his painting. Wilhelm Hausenstein wrote about Vallotton's *Baigneuses* in 1918, "When a style is so enormously strong like the style of this woodcut vignette then it conveys more than book illustration. It conveys the complete taste of an age — of a future."

In Germany, journal editorial offices became meeting places of graphic producing artists: In Munich the magazine *Jugend* and the *Insel* as well as the illustrated humorous review *Simplizissimus*, in Berlin *Pan*. In all these offices young forces were active, urging for new designs in the artistic scene.

*Pan* thanks its graphic design to Otto Eckmann from Hamburg. He found a style for the magazine which could be described as aristocratic. He stylized mainly flower and animal motifs by combining their grace with pure linear ornamentation. His frames and vignettes have a very noble effect and there is no sign of overdone frills. The writing which Eckmann designed is still used today as classical Jugendstil writing.

Chief editors of the journal were Julius Meier-Graefe and Otto Julius Bierbaum, the poet. Meier-Graefe brought his international connections into the publishing office so that *Pan* had horizons covering home and abroad. On the other hand, the rather complicated finance structure brought problems to the exquisitely designed journal. Partners in the magazine were practically members of German high finance who naturally had the tendency to give the journal a certain elitist course. Because of this Bierbaum soon left the editorial staff. He did not believe that the magazine's ideas could be realized, "because they were based on an over-estimation of the German upper middle class. There are not a thousand people amongst them who will support an art which lives from development." Pan is "a journal for millionaires, a journal which is not to be read but only placed on a table in a room in which people of taste and intellectuality are danced attendance on — it has then already fulfilled its purpose".

The pattern of the magazine *Jugend* which appeared from 1896 was completely different. The ductus of the Jugend was not clear from the first day on but instead editors and illustrating artists first gropingly approached their style. However, a title picture from Ludwig von Zumbusch which represented Georg Hirth's slogan "youth be a watchword" had a signal effect. Hirth was an experienced publisher. He had already assured himself a considerable collection of patterns for graphic artists and substantial editorial and production knowledge with his very successful "abundance of forms". His *Jugend* could now come up with a novelty. He had discovered a possibility of backing parts of the drawings with coloured areas which gave them a stronger effect from a distance and considerably increased the graphic fascination of the works. The *Simplizissimus* very soon followed the example and adopted the new graphic process.

The *Jugend* became a veritable reservoir of Jugendstil artists without being the true voice of the innovators. It was never opinion forming, however, it offered the possibility to work in the new style. It wanted to replace the existing boredom in the magazine sector in literal and pictorial design. "Youth. The word was a programme! More than that! Fanfare! One only had to call, paint, write, live! And to receive joy and malcontent, charm and brashness, hope and fulfillment." (A. de Nora) The *Hamburger Nachrichten* wrote, "The Munich Jugend has conquered the world in the short period of its existence. It has all the characteristics of a conquerer: spirit and strength, daring boldness and a divine impertinence; it bangs on the thick heads of the Philistines, thumbs its nose at academic ardour and the antiquated scholarship; it laughs and ridicules the intolerables of art and life; it spreads its gags on the honourable bald heads of pedantic narrow-minded people."

*Simplizissimus* was founded in Munich several months after *Jugend*. This was a review which was completely dedicated to humour and only occasionally showed Art Nouveau tendencies. It had a very limited thematic circle and as we know today, the editors had the constant fear that the continued repetition of similar jokes would eventually begin to annoy the (obviously indulgent) readers. However, the *Simplizissimus* had a speciality, but this was not in the artistic field: its humour was especially biting to the authorities, and the public prosecutor was a frequent visitor because of lese majesty and similar delicts. Publishers and editors quite often worked under unusual circumstances from abroad because they had to avoid imprisonment. But prison terms could not bend its sarcasm, it only fell victim to the regime of National Socialism.

The third Munich journal, the *Insel* was produced by two cousins from Bremen who moved to Munich. The two editors Alfred Walter Heymel and Rudolf Alexander Schröder wanted to realize a long-desired childhood dream. They also brought in Julius Bierbaum who had left his position with *Pan*. Heymel's considerable fortune enabled them to publish the magazine in a technically very attractive design. The Insel's editorial programme was committed to a "regeneration of the German conscience" and it was a distinct literary publication. However, the few illustrations are today of great importance. As well as Th. Th. Heine who also belonged to *Simplizissimus* and *Jugend*, the young Markus Behmer stood out for his perfectly drawn disturbing fantasies.

Admittedly the publication was denied any notable publishing or economic success. It was published for three years with great financial concessions from Heymel, but eventually closed because of the complete lack of public interest. However, it was the beginning of the Insel Verlag which was later to become world-famous. The editor Heymel had R. A. Schröder design and build him an exceptional flat which became a meeting place for the people from Schwabing. Their uprightness caused Th. Th. Heine to say, "Goethe could have died here". There is a short report which shows the joy of life in artistry in those days. Heine describes a Heymel evening, "Everything was tremendously tasteful. The food was served on old Meissen porcelain with pure gold cutlery which had, however, been silver-plated to avoid anything which hinted at nouveau riche. One talked all the time about Goethe and felt that one was very exclusive. I couldn't stand it anymore. Something had to happen. With a quick decision I placed a piece of beef in my mouth

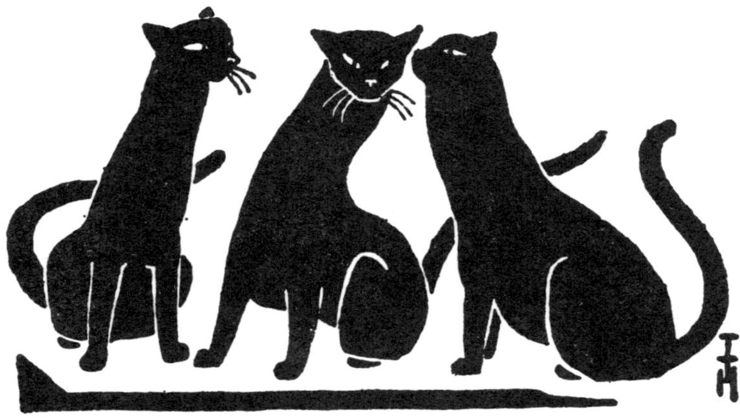

with a knife. Alfred Kubin who sat opposite me called out loud, 'Heine ate with a knife, halloo!' Then he jumped up and danced wildly with Saharet who had, until then, sat, bored, beside Heymel . . ."

The illustrated book and, as an innovation, the dust-jacket with Art Nouveau motifs which Albert Langen introduced for his books were very important in Germany. However, there was the great danger that the contents of a book were disregarded in favour of the design. "Around 1900 the beautiful book was mentioned more than the good book. The illustrative and decorative accessories of a book were often more important than the contents or the style of the author; change in accent from books as literary to books as graphic art can be detected." (Simon)

Stanley Weintraub passed down an anecdote about the cynics Oscar Wilde and Ada Leverson. She suggested that he should bring out a book which only contained pages with decorative margins. Full of beautiful unwritten thoughts, on Japanese paper and expensively bound in green leather, it should be a limited numbered work of art, very rare. Wilde agreed, "it should be dedicated to you", he said to her, "and the unwritten text shall be illustrated by Aubrey Beardsley. We need 500 copies for good friends and one for America".

A typical example is offered by the brilliant draughtsman Thomas Theodor Heine who illustrated a book called *Die Barrisons* which appeared in 1897 by Schuster and Löffler, the publishers of *Pan*. This book is a fascinating document of Art Nouveau in book art, a monument of design — and a completely trivial text about the most popular revue girls in those days. Heine had also created pictures for *Pan*, but above all he designed book jackets for Albert Langen and sketches for *Simplizissimus*. He was one of the most active and stimulating illustrators of Art Nouveau. He remained with Simplizissimus until the takeover of power by the National Socialists in 1933 forced him to flee the country, as he was one of the most hated publishers in those circles. He died in Stockholm in 1948 as a highly respected artist in Sweden.

J. R. Witzel was a genius in the field of linear art. Paper margins were no limit for him, he cut into the edges of his drawings with such unique elegance that the viewer automatically includes the space around the drawing.

Another draughtsman deserves mention: Baron Hans Henning Voigt who worked under the pseudonym Alastair. He was clearly influenced by Beardsley and created a decadent fin de siècle style to which he remained true for the rest of his life and which brought him international acclaim. He also arranged his life just as he sketched. The tendency to eroticism in Art Nouveau was cultivated by quite a few artists in Munich in those days. For example Franz Blei's Publications which published a magazine with erotic works for a short time and *Die Auster* whose leading draughtsman was Franz von Bayros. However, all of these publications were only available to a small circle and were limited to a small edition of numbered bibliophile copies.

The transfiguration to a symbol is a phenomenon which we come across everywhere in Art Nouveau graphic art in Austria. "The artists did not wrack their brains over what was symbolical or allegorical. They were certain that art had to express great, holy ideas, that it had to entice the secrets and ideas from nature. Their area of living was an ideal world, one higher than the day to day world. What was new here and in other places (in painting) with Böcklin or Klinger or Stuck or Khnopff was the transfiguration to a symbol, to the sublime, to something out of the ordinary, the universal validity, philosophical and universally humaneness which goes above every particular instance."

*Ver Sacrum* — Holy Spring, was the title of a magazine from the Viennese Secession and, at the same time, the artists' programme — the key word of art in the country in those days. Viennese artists around 1900 wished to give their art a frank and open expression, they wanted to awaken the feeling of truth and beauty through their work. High artistic demands went along with this and often the greatest achievements were made in graphic art because it was more self-contained.

An especially Austrian and Viennese style of art arose. The city offered a very special spiritual climate for the development. In Munich it was the free sense of gaiety which invited artists, but in Vienna it was psychoanalysis, which was discovered in Vienna for a good reason. "Freud's psychoanalysis stimulated the whole of cultural life, however, this was not a science connected with the problems of everyday life but one closely associated with the needs and concerns of people and their era. That it could, had to and did originate in Vienna, already characterizes the mental state of this metropolis, which on the one hand is clear-sighted and on the other hand disguises its repressed desires in symbols." The picture world of Art Nouveau came completely from this world.

The *Secession*, which had been formed in Vienna within the framework of the *Austrian Union of Graphic Artists*, became the reservoir for all creative forces in the country. It also attempted to establish contacts with like-minded artists in other countries. The magazine *Ver Sacrum* became its mouthpiece. Above all artists of Art Nouveau printing gathered in the editorial offices of this publication. An exceptionally rigid, self-willed style of geometric and ornamental components arose. "We want an art which does not serve foreign interests but which is also without fear or hate of anything foreign. Art from other countries should stimulate us to reflect upon ourselves, we want to recognize and admire it for what it is worth, but we do not want to imitate it." This appeared in the first issue of *Ver Sacrum*, and they really did succeed in following this line. Impressionism and Symbolism, Japanese art and Northerners, Segantini, Hodler, van Gogh, Cézanne and Seurat could be seen in Vienna beside artists from Austria.

In 1903 another union of artists appeared in public. It was mainly the same people who had been with the Secession, but who had left due to differences of opinion. Now they came together for the foundation of the *Wiener Werkstätten* which also produced some remarkable examples of graphic art. The outstanding leader was Gustav Klimt, an important painter who had also created a great graphic oeuvre which is distinguished by the individual character of his style of drawing. This style was carried on by his pupil Egon Schiele while as a painter he rapidly developed further than his tutor. Finally Oskar Kokoschka should be mentioned as a graphic artist, especially for his work with the Wiener Werkstätten. He and Egon Schiele created the bridge from Art Nouveau to Austrian Expressionism.

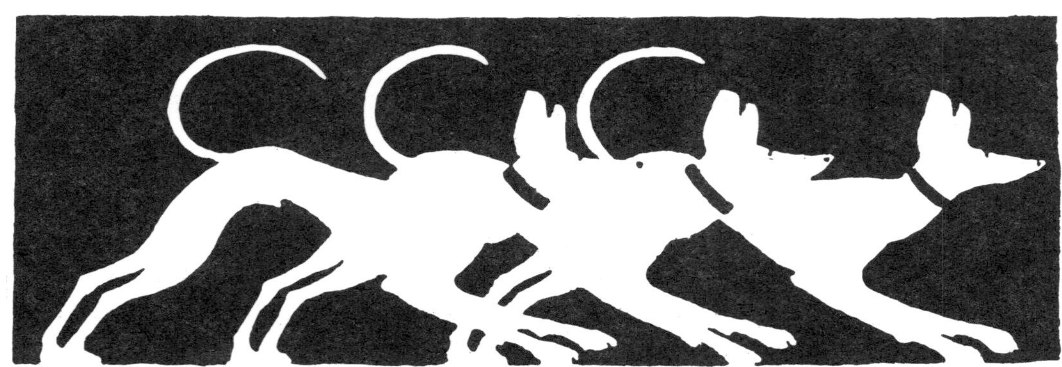

# ILLUSTRATIONS

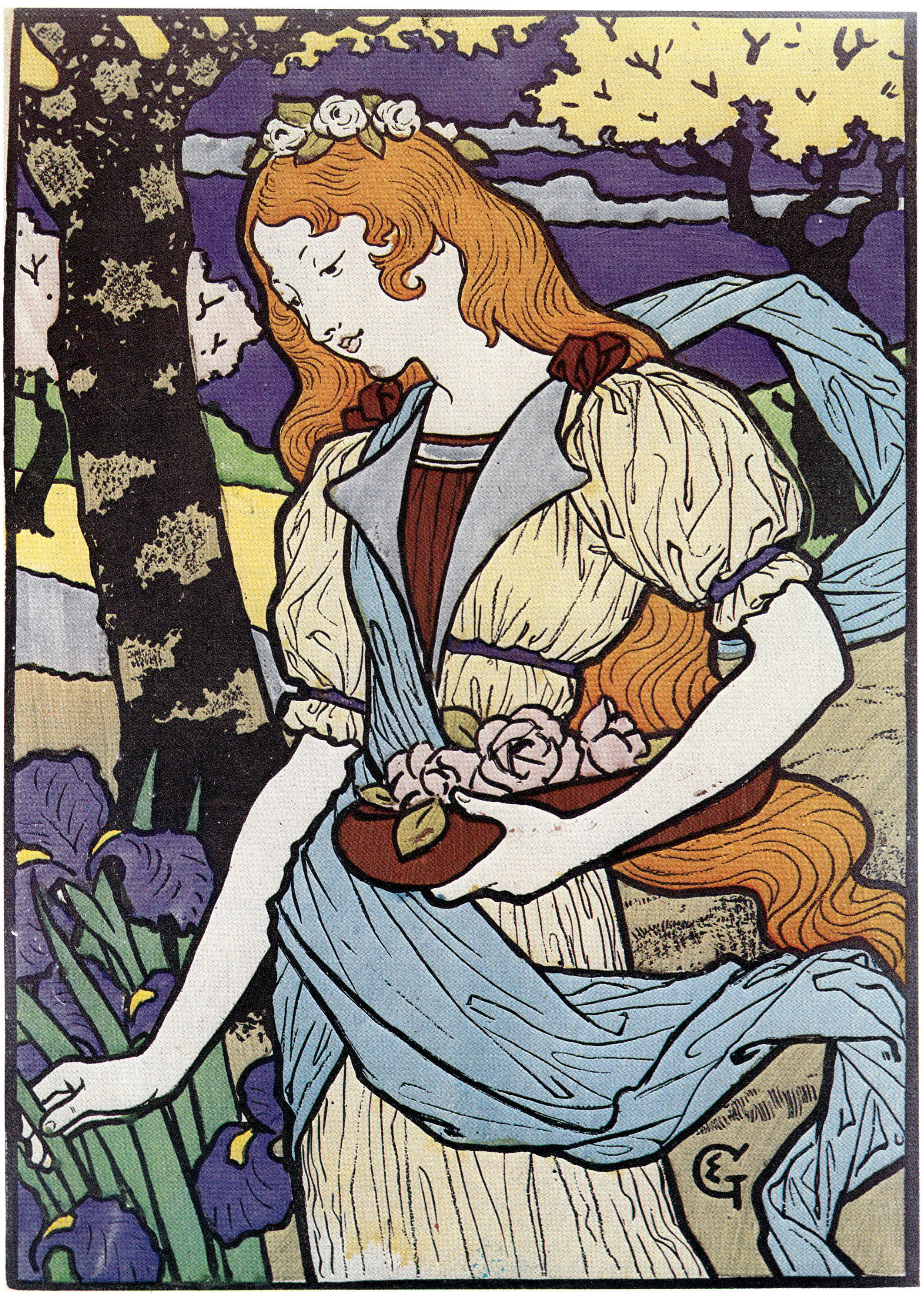

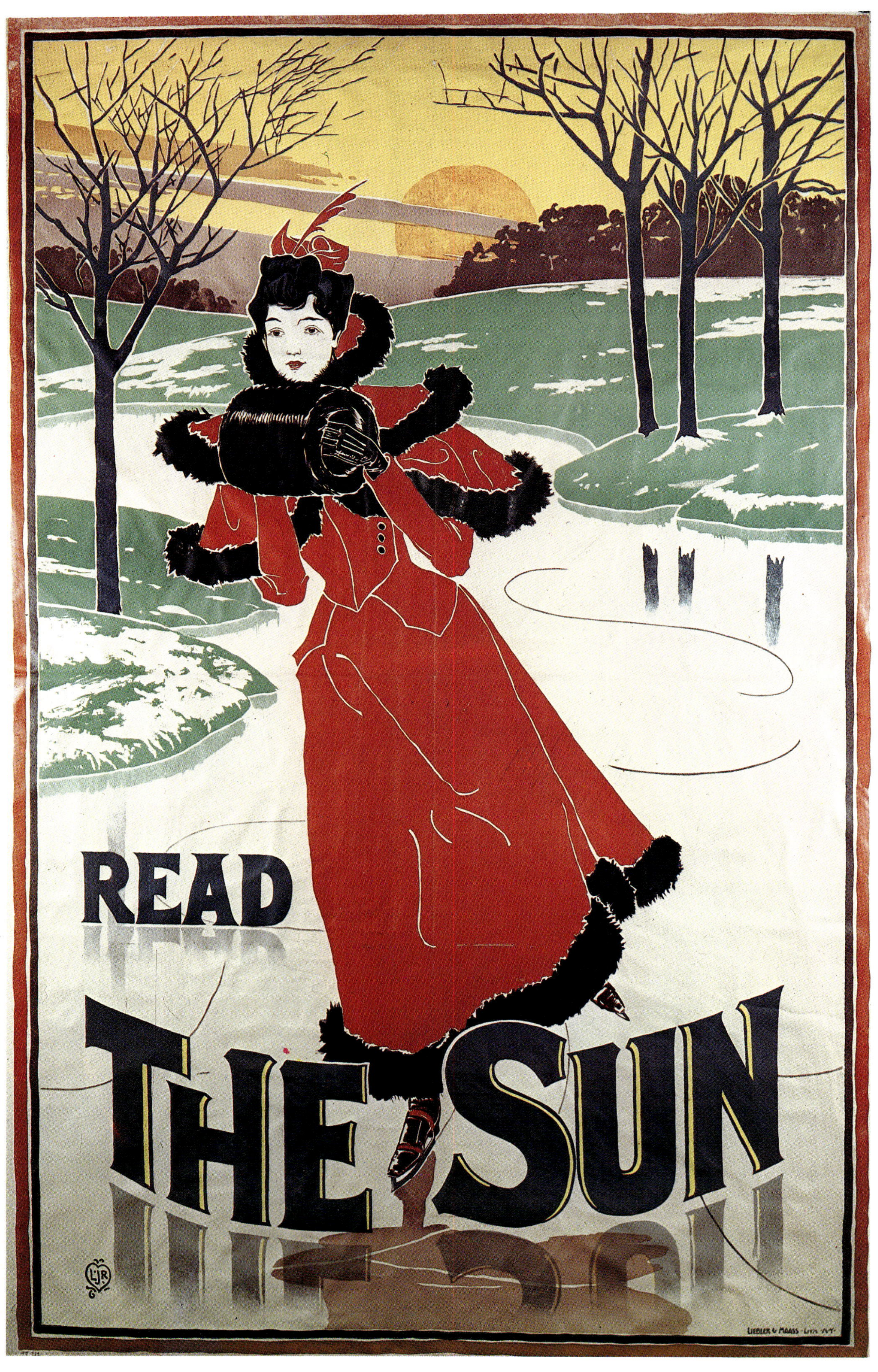
READ
THE SUN
LIEBLER & MAASS · LITH · N.Y.

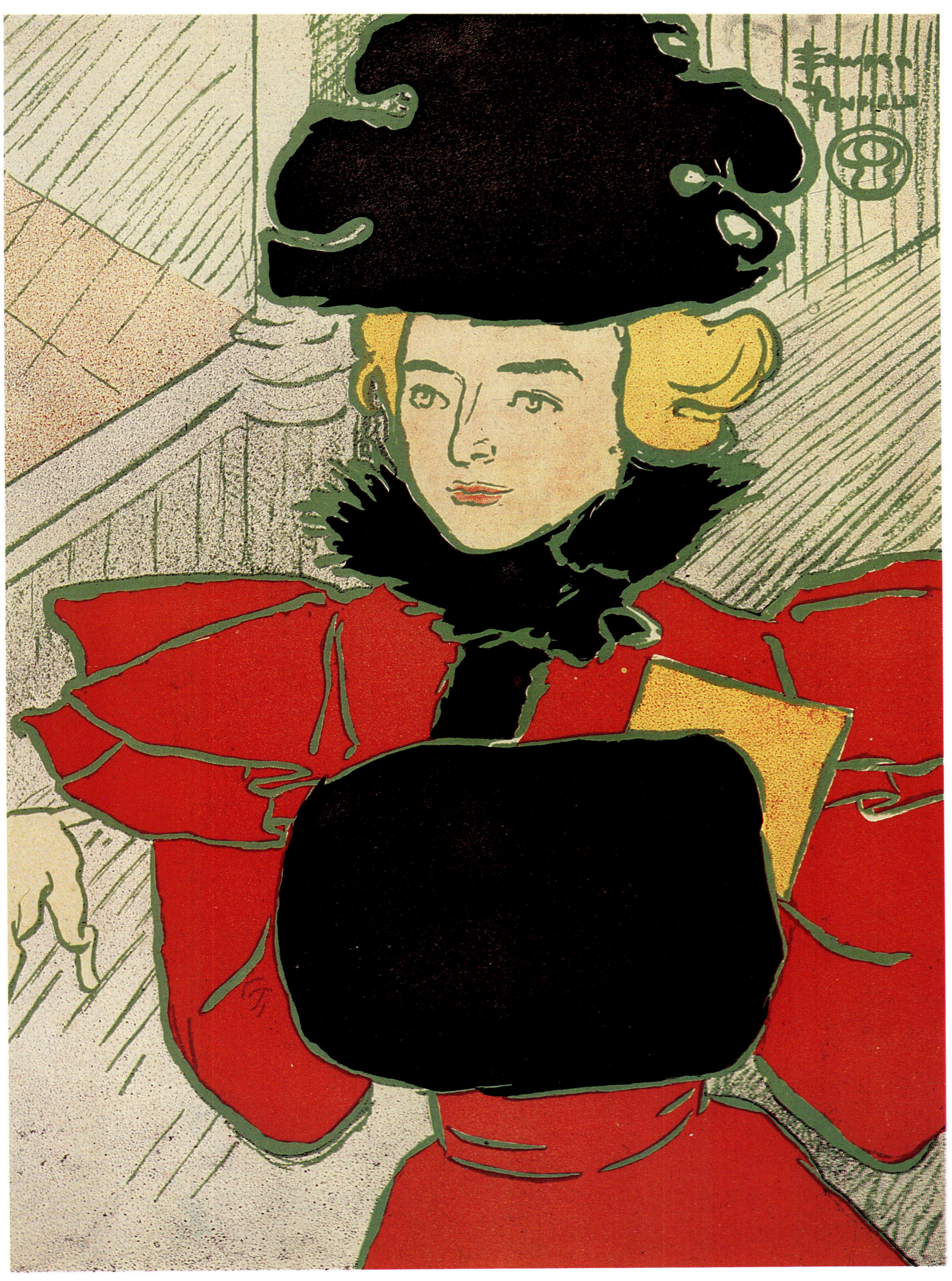

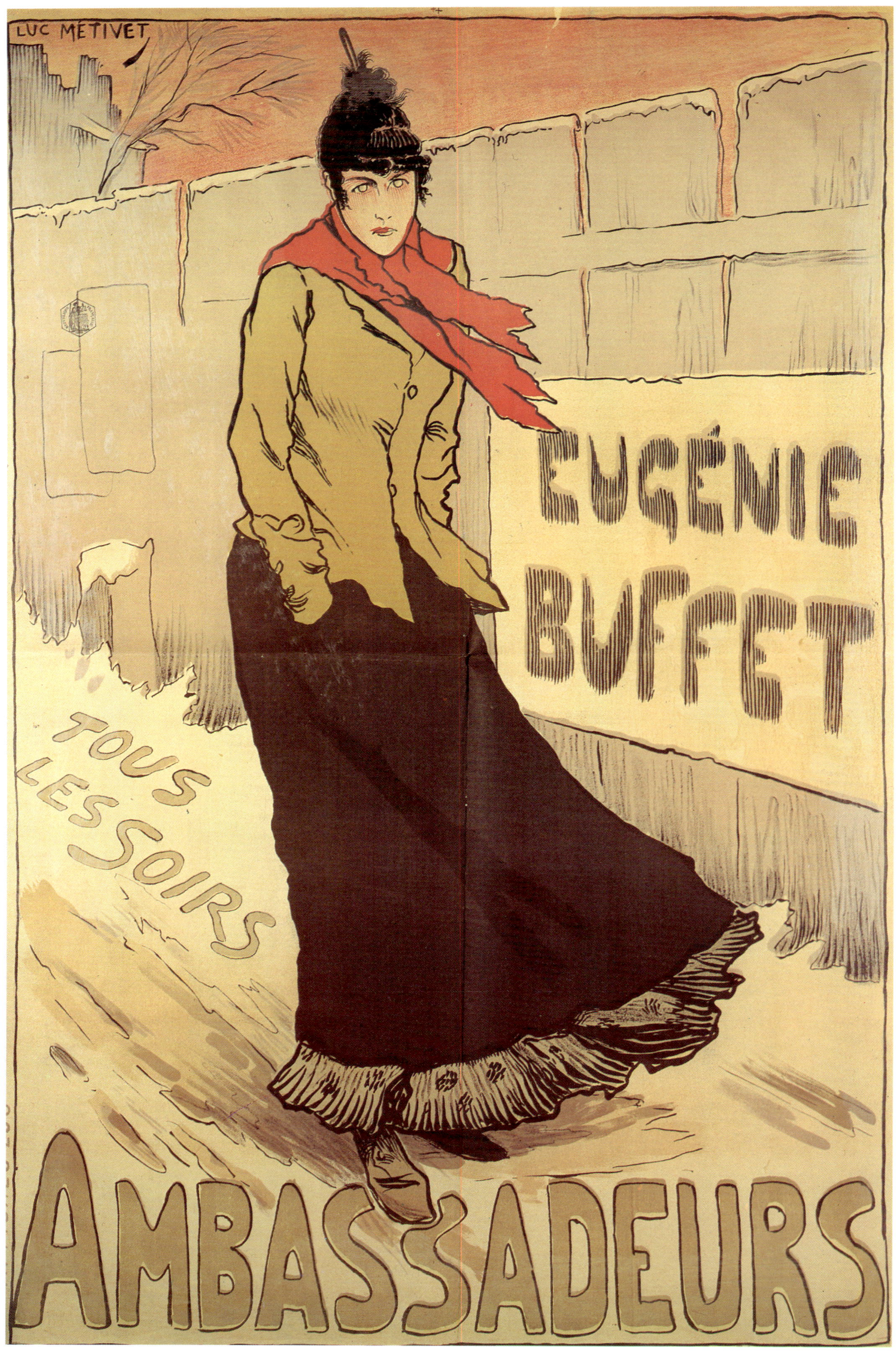
LUC MÉTIVET
EUGÉNIE
BUFFET
TOUS
LES SOIRS
AMBASSADEURS

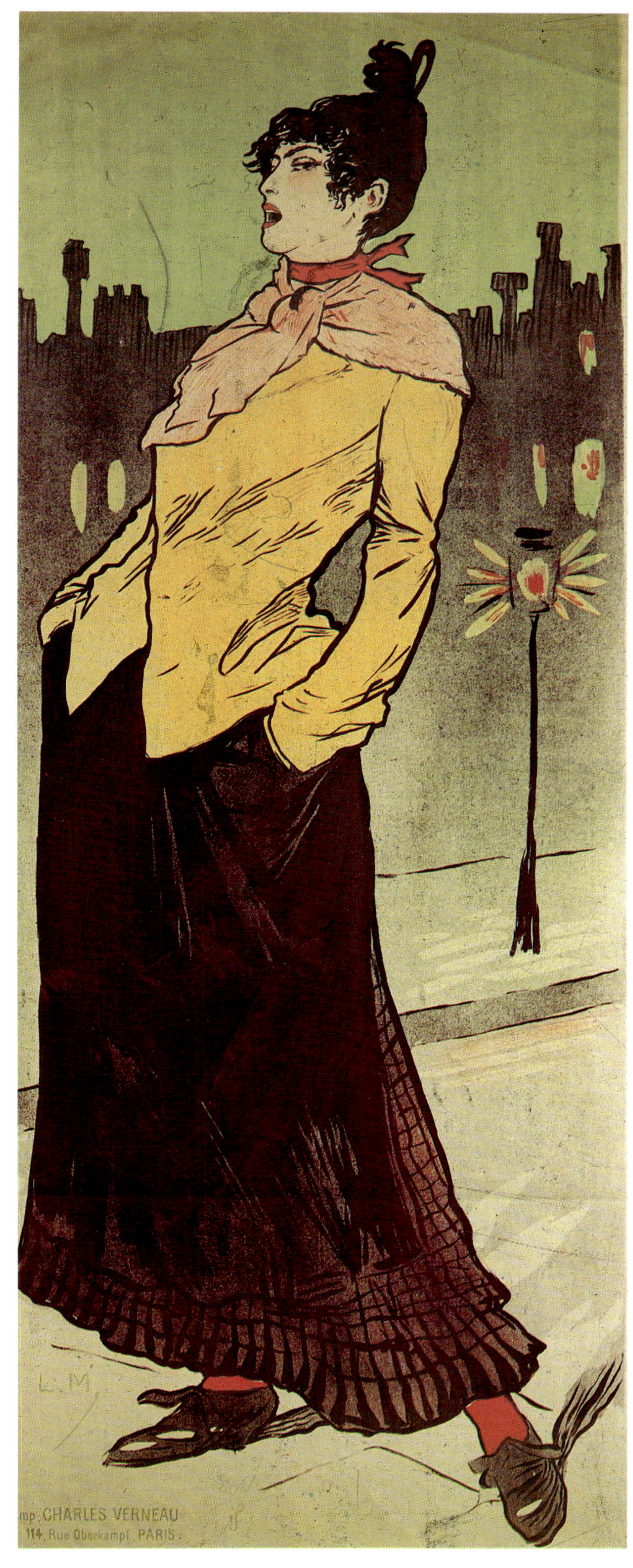
L.M
mp. CHARLES VERNEAU
114, Rue Oberkampf, PARIS

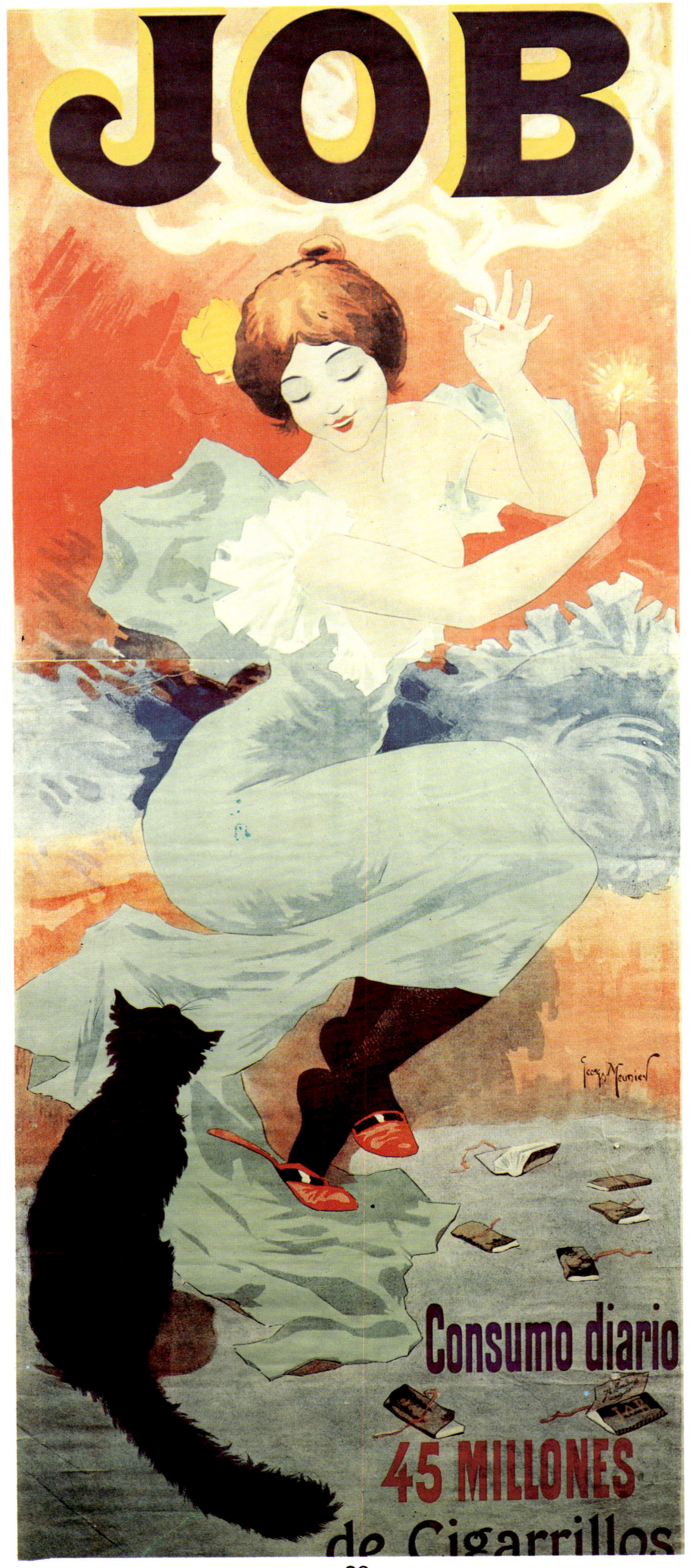
JOB
Consumo diario
45 MILLONES
de Cigarrillos

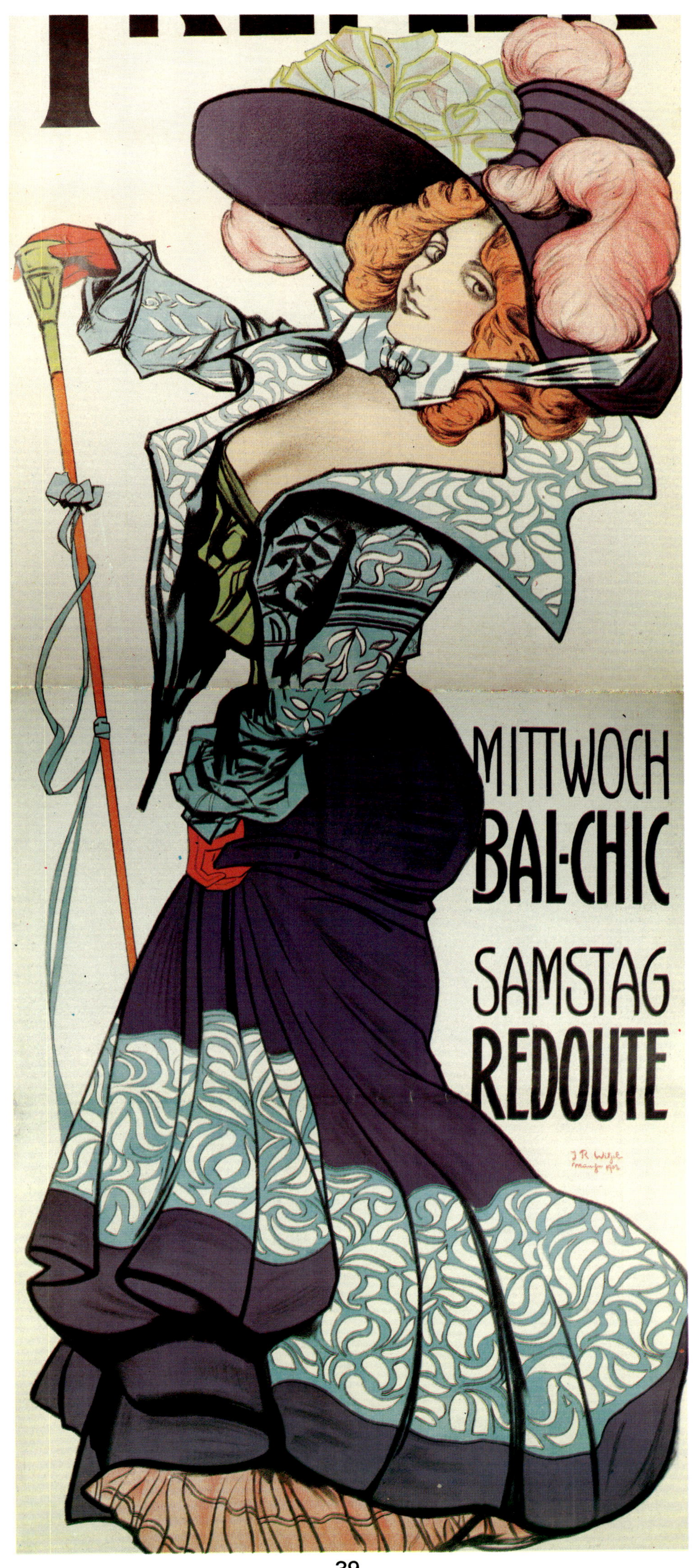
MITTWOCH
BAL-CHIC
SAMSTAG
REDOUTE

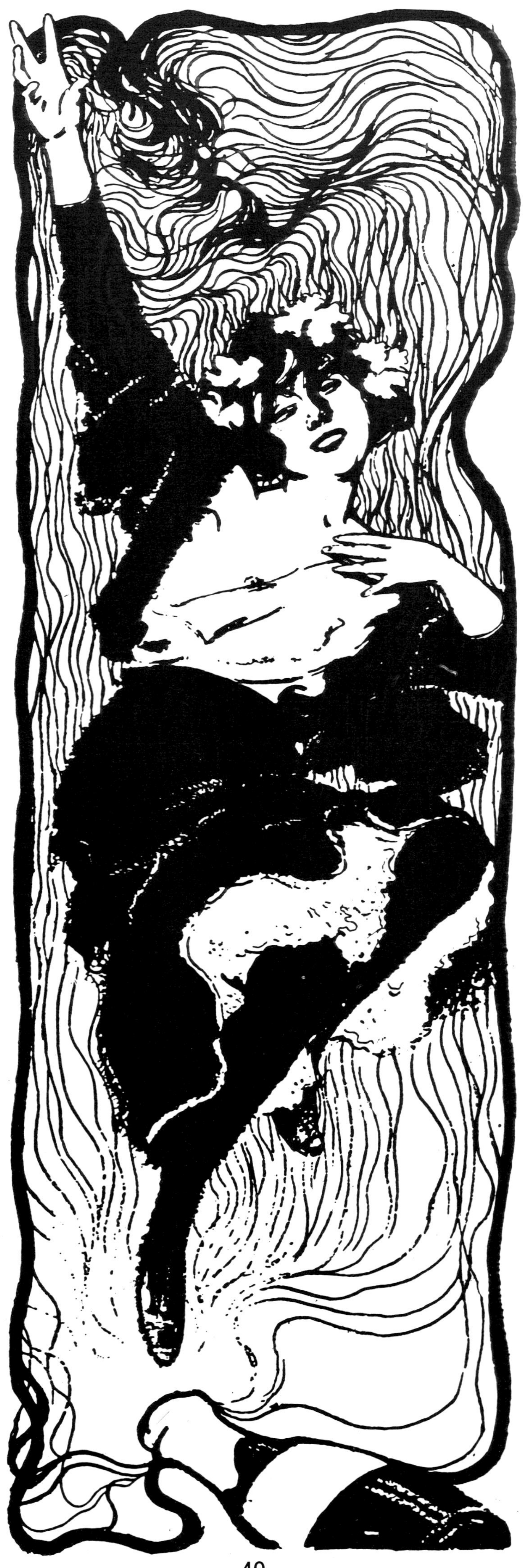

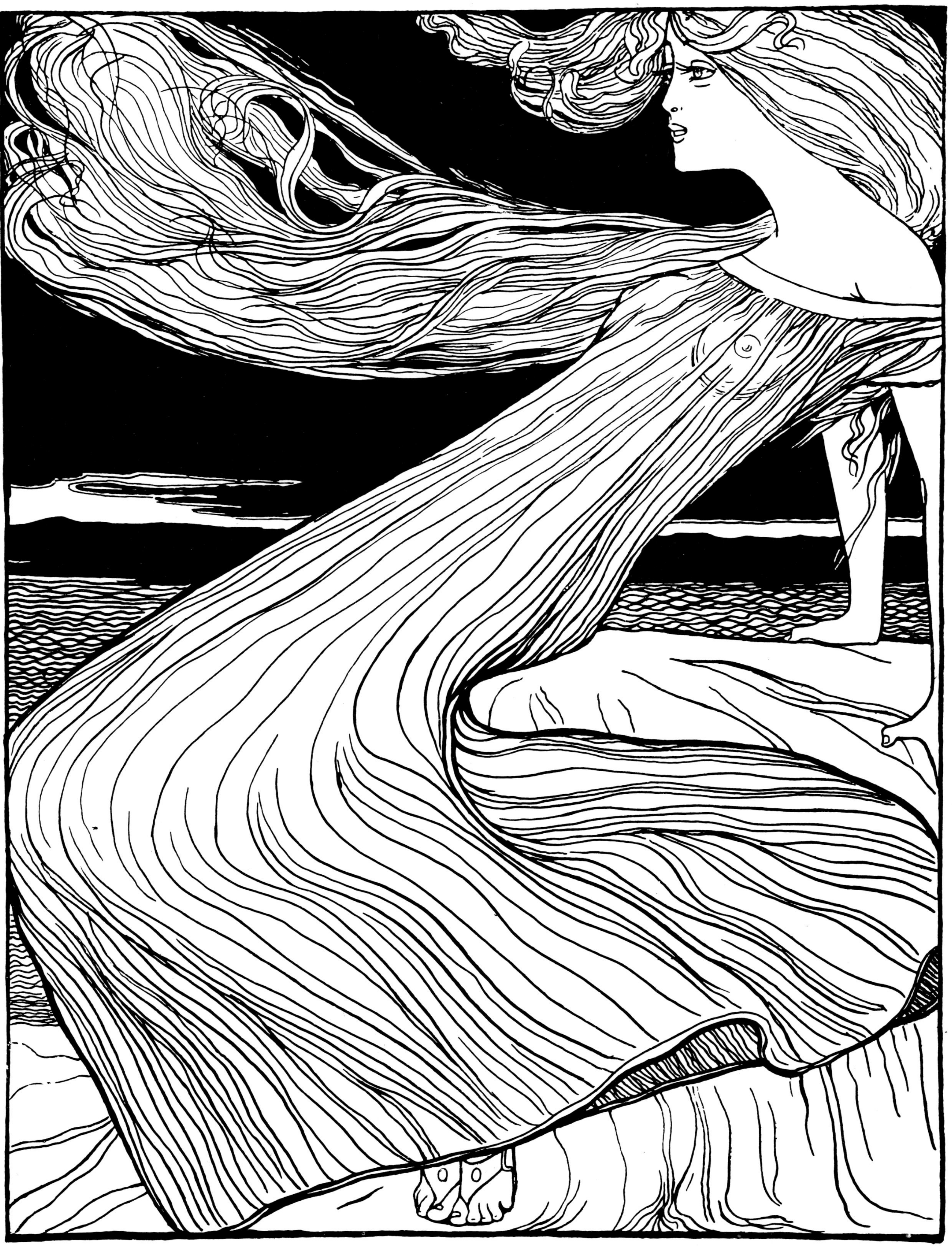

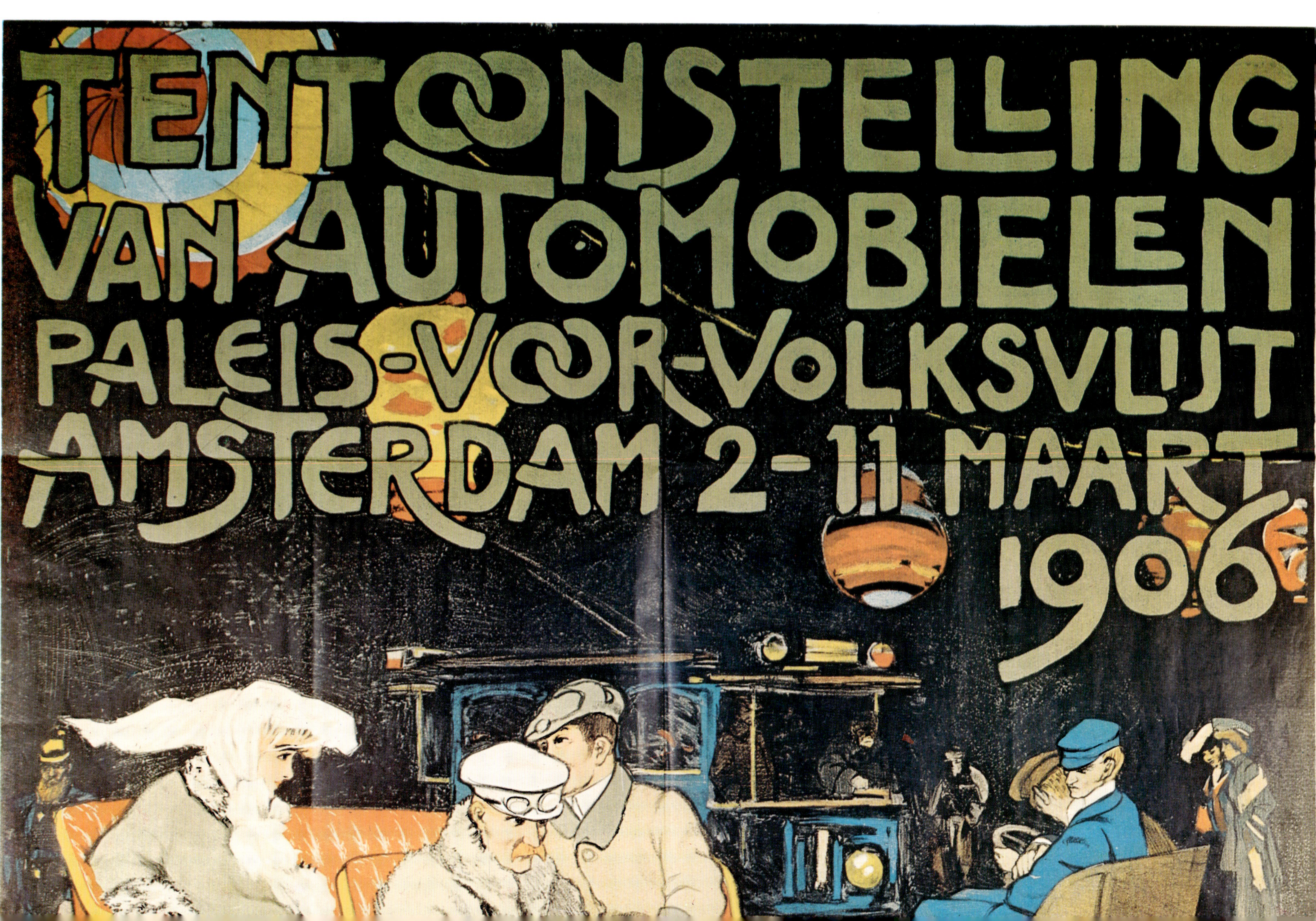
TENTOONSTELLING
VAN AUTOMOBIELEN
PALEIS-VOOR-VOLKSVLIJT
AMSTERDAM 2-11 MAART
1906

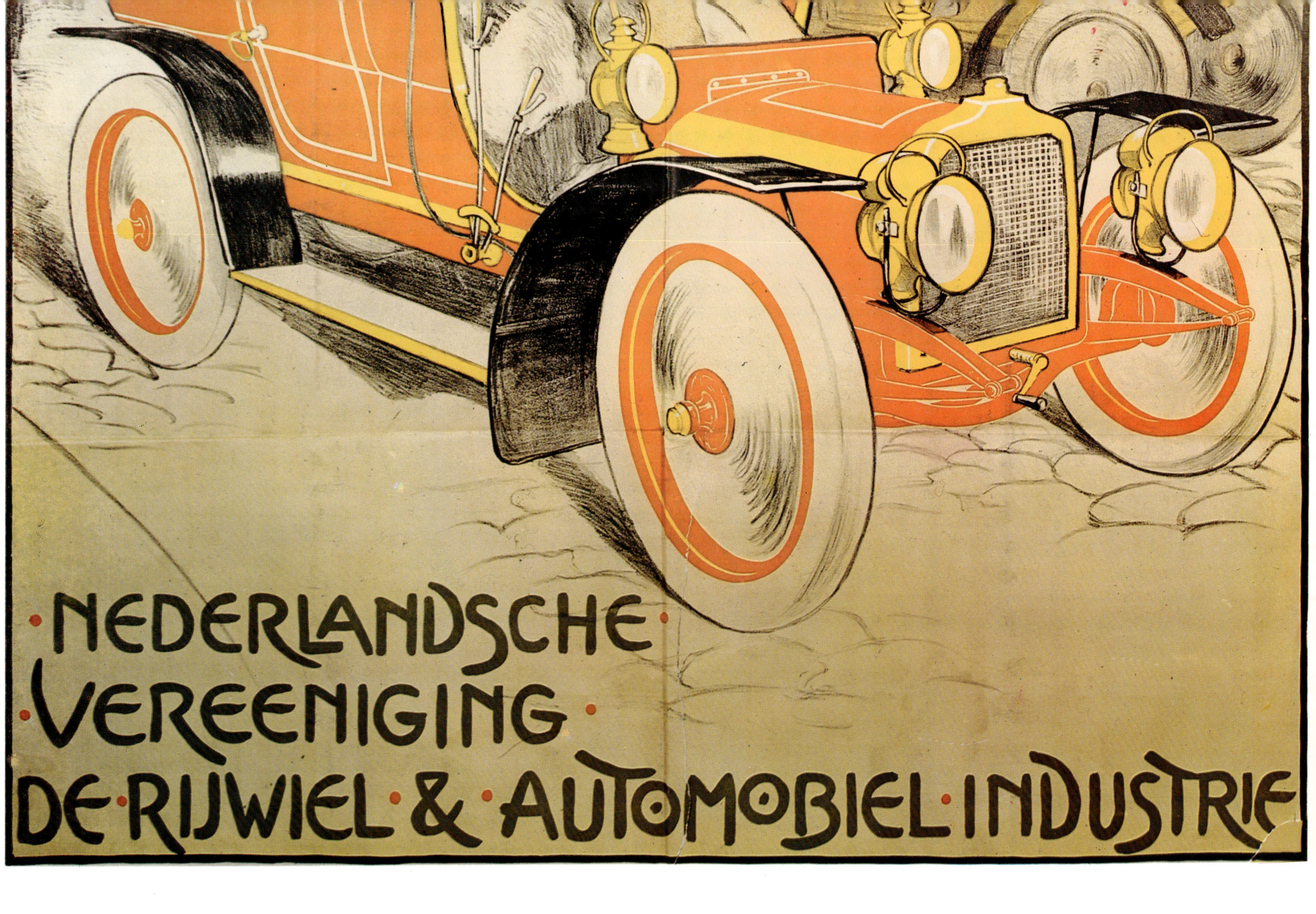
·NEDERLANDSCHE·
·VEREENIGING·
DE·RIJWIEL·&·AUTOMOBIEL·INDUSTRIE

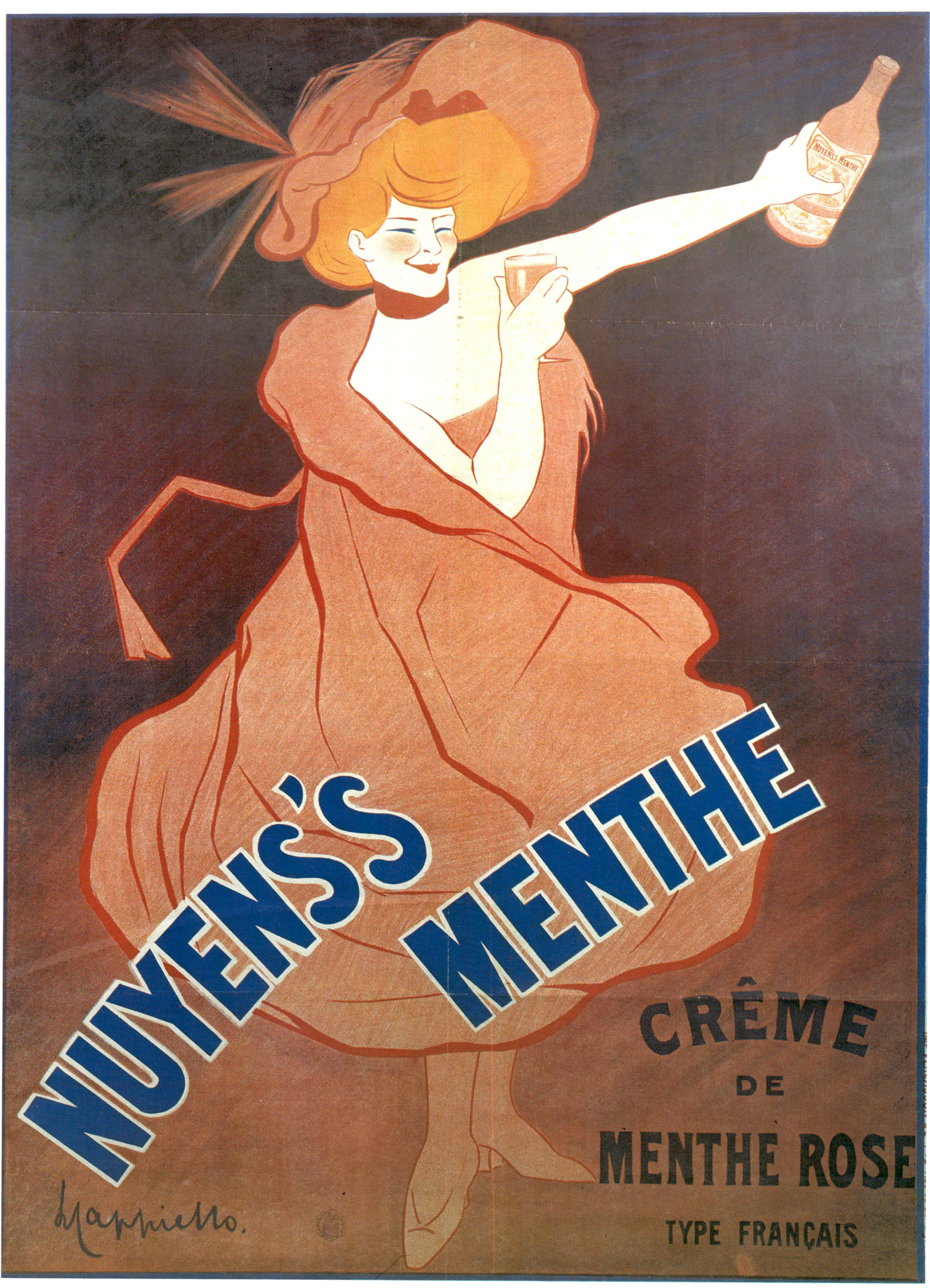
NUYENS'S MENTHE
CRÊME
DE
MENTHE ROSE
TYPE FRANÇAIS
LCappiello.

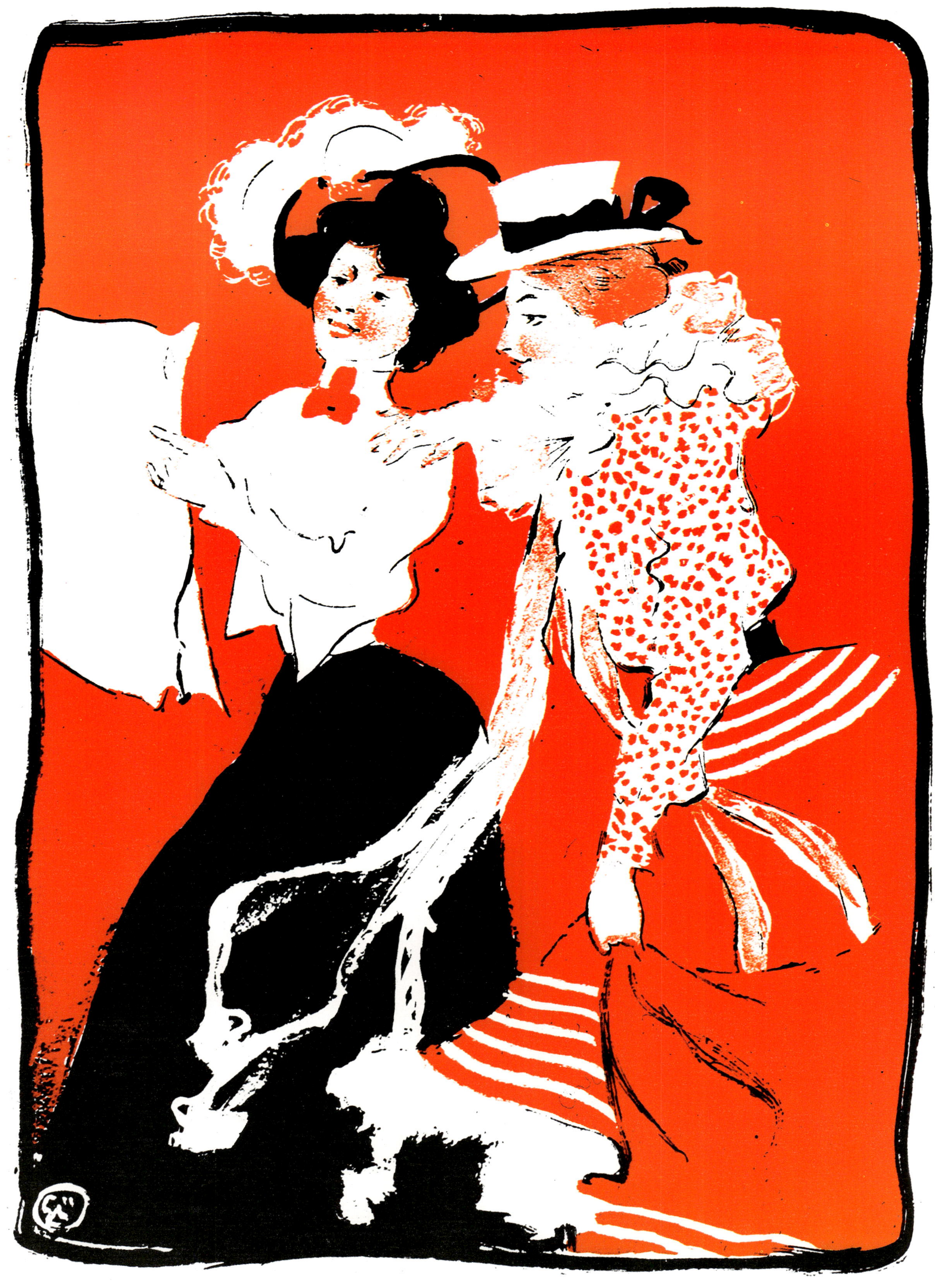

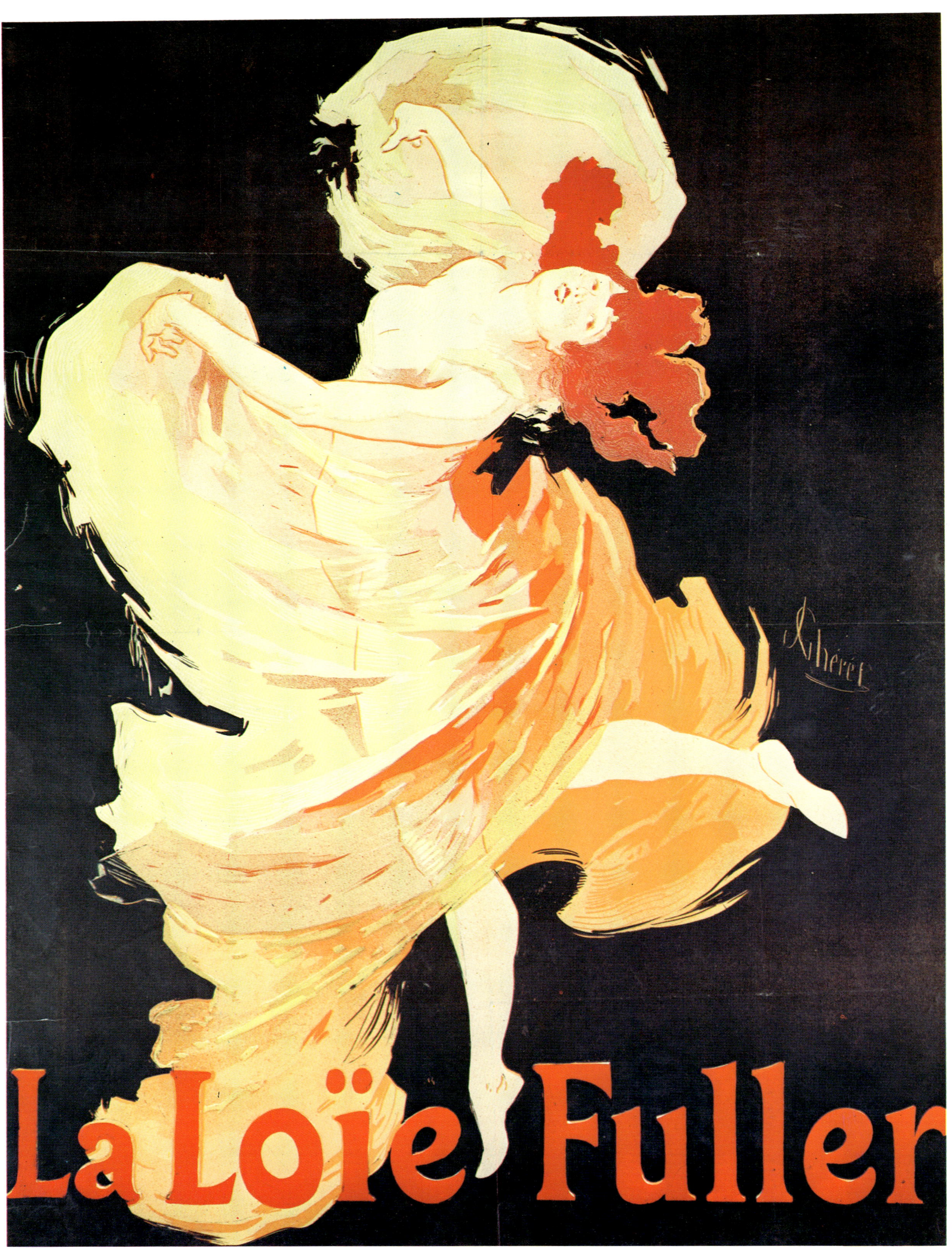
Chéret
La Loïe Fuller

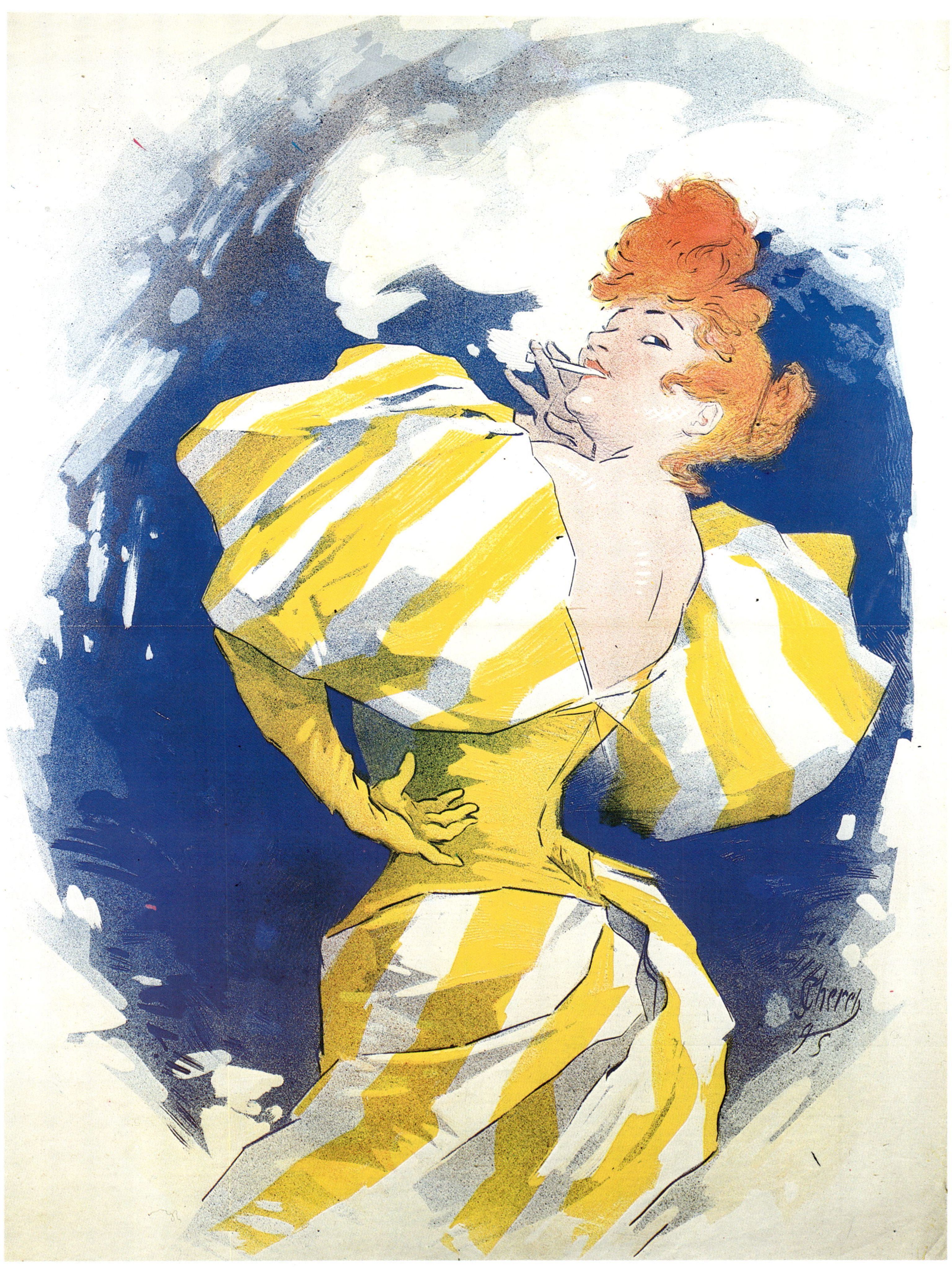
Chéret
95

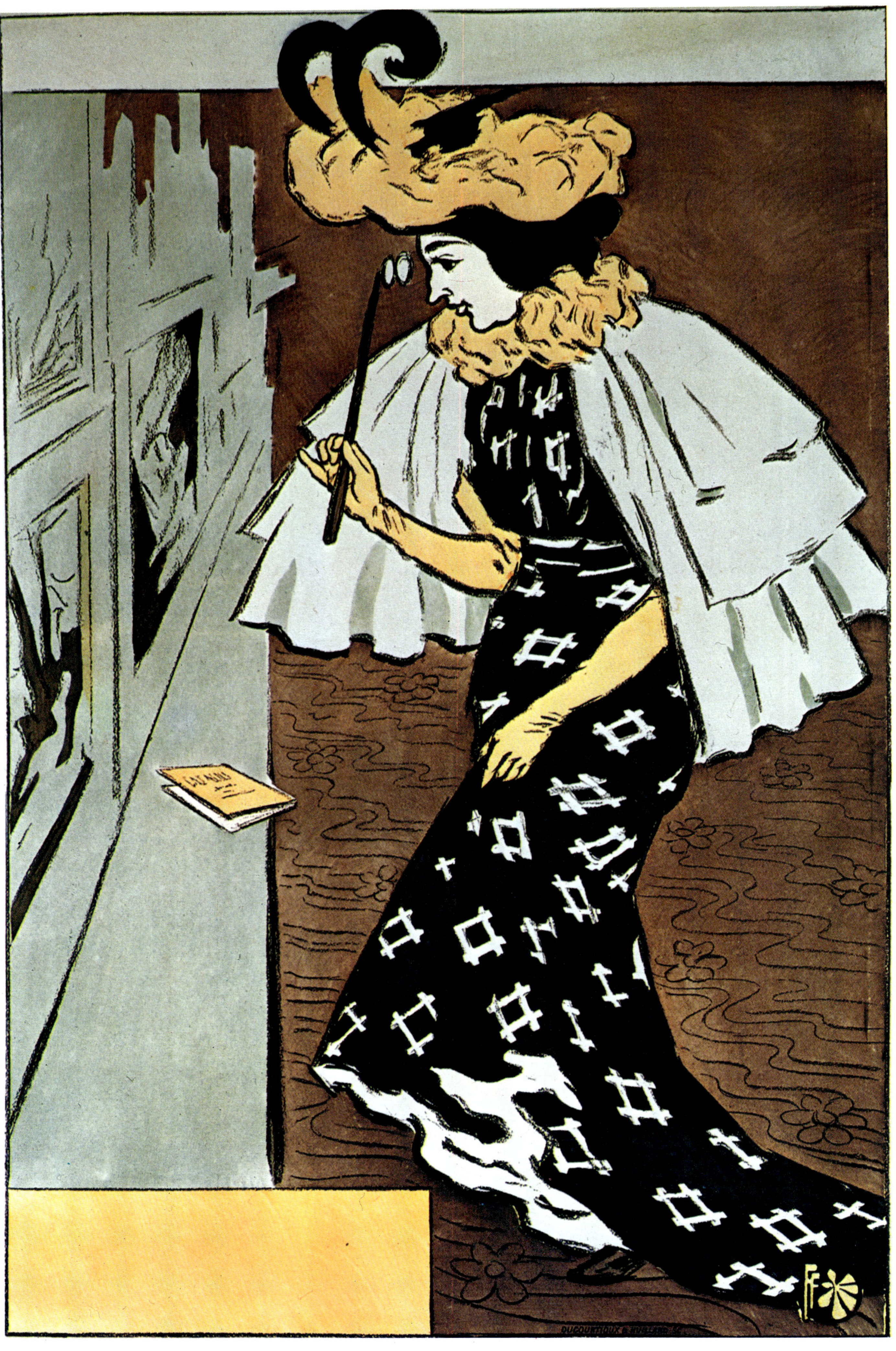

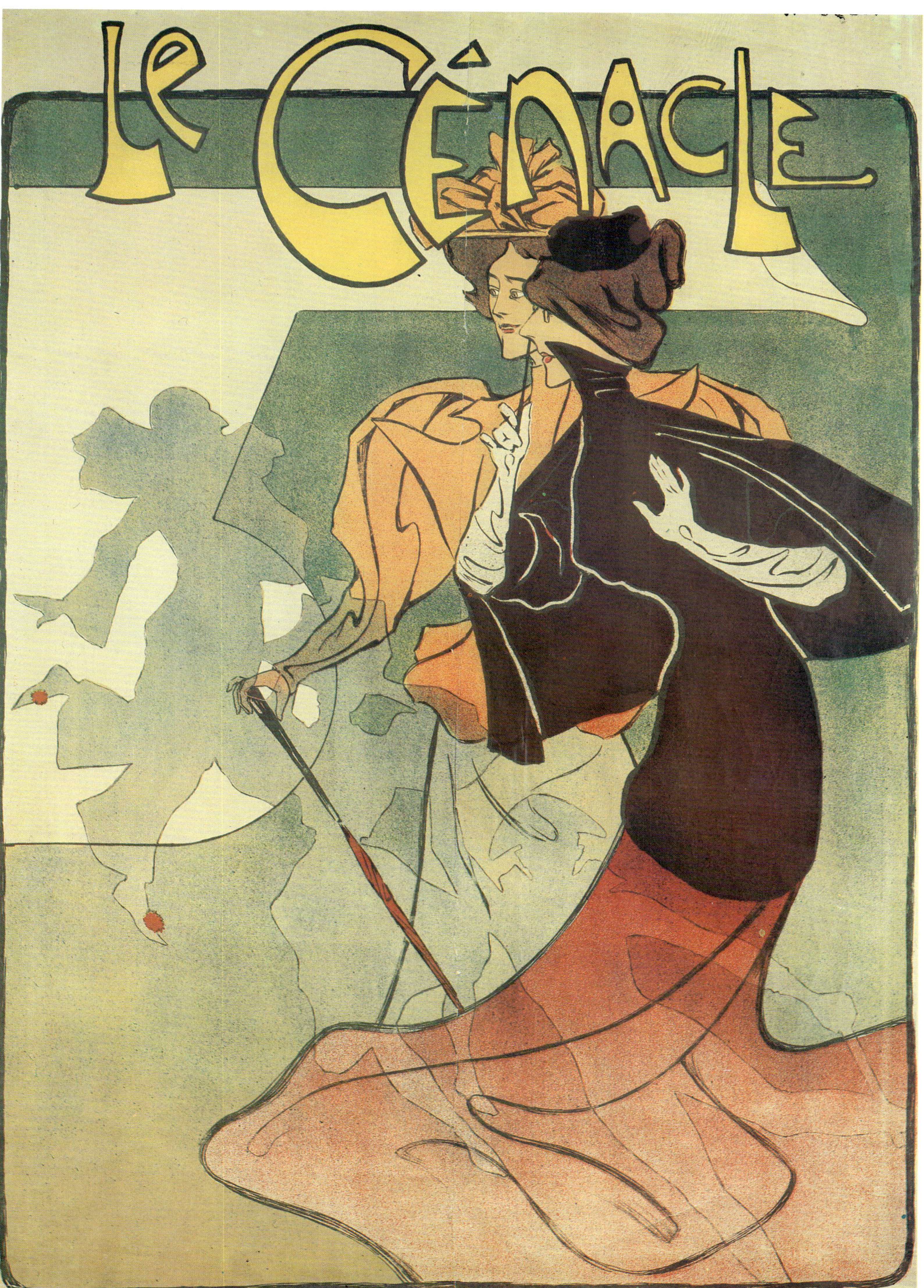
LE CÉNACLE

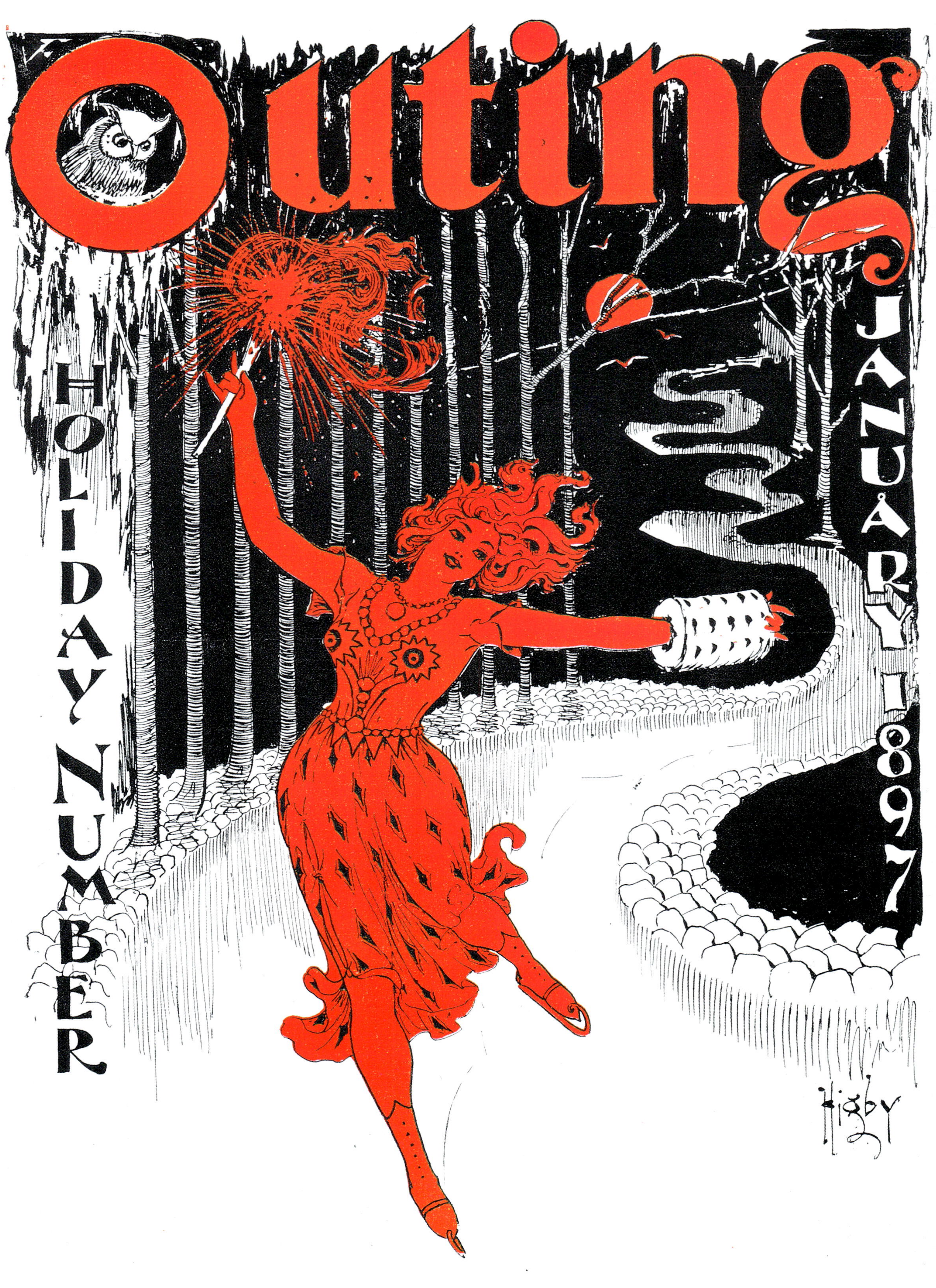
Outing
HOLIDAY NUMBER
JANUARY 1897
Higby

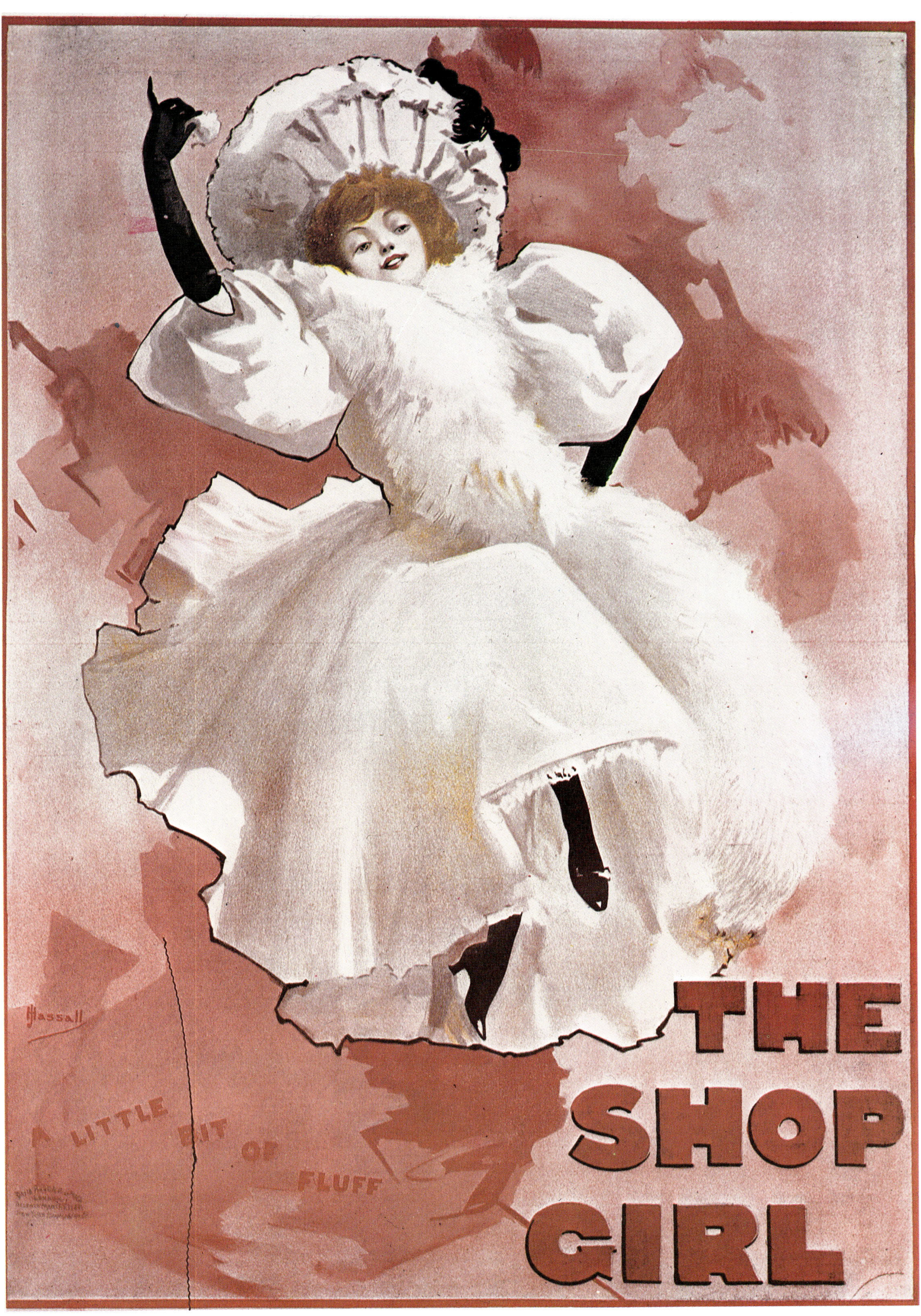
Hassall
A LITTLE BIT OF FLUFF
THE SHOP GIRL

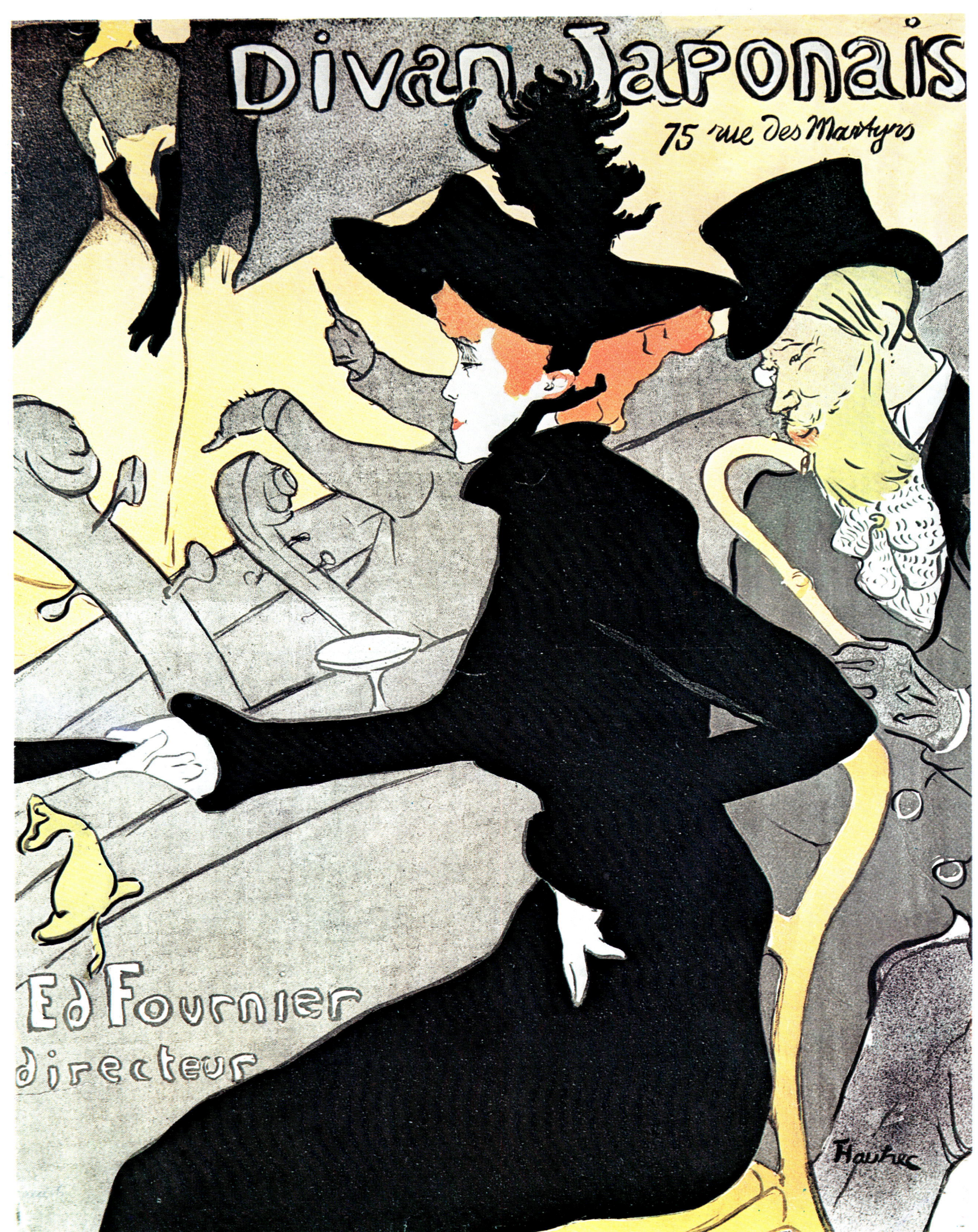
Divan Japonais
75 rue des Martyrs
Ed Fournier
directeur
T-Lautrec

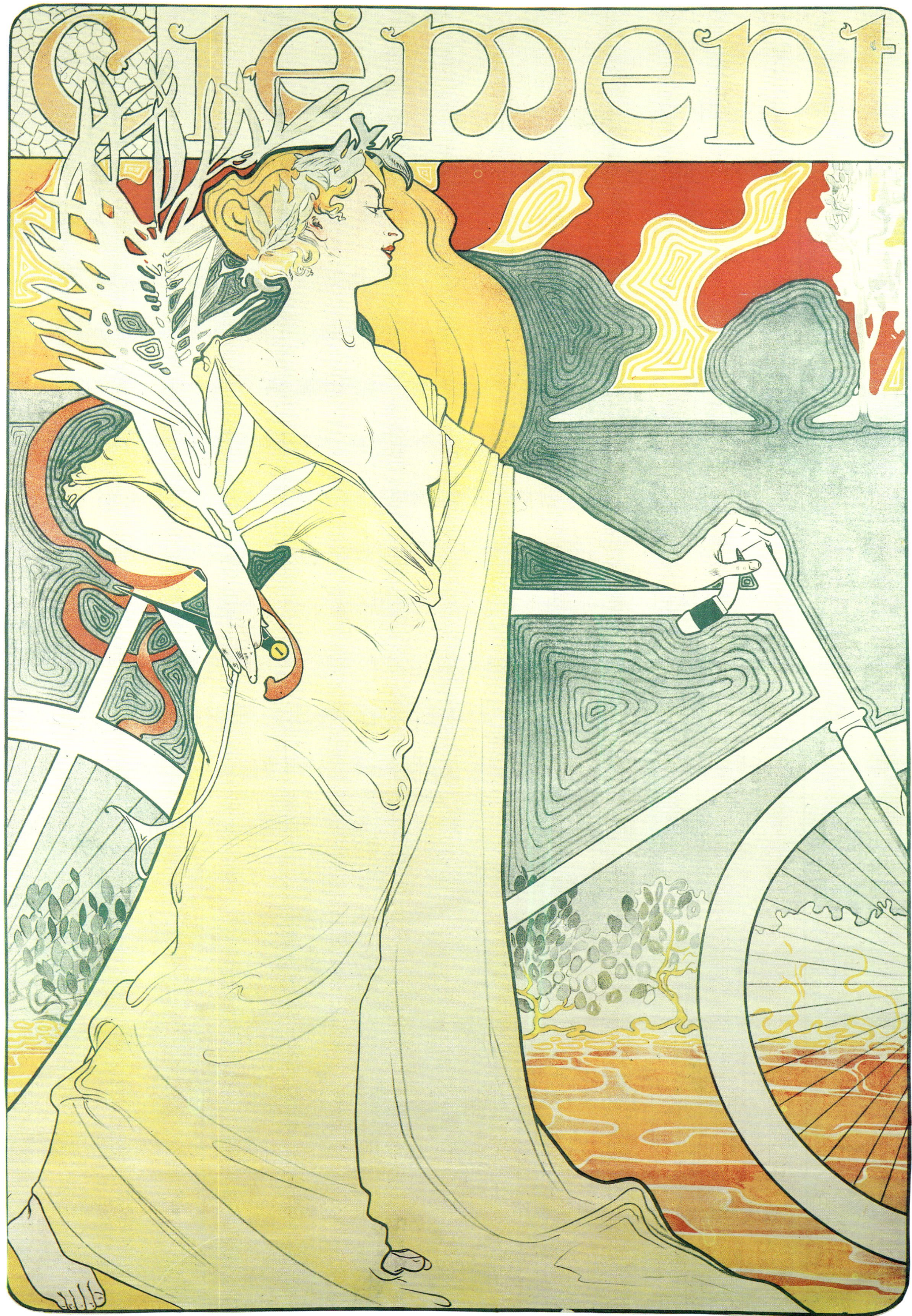
Clément

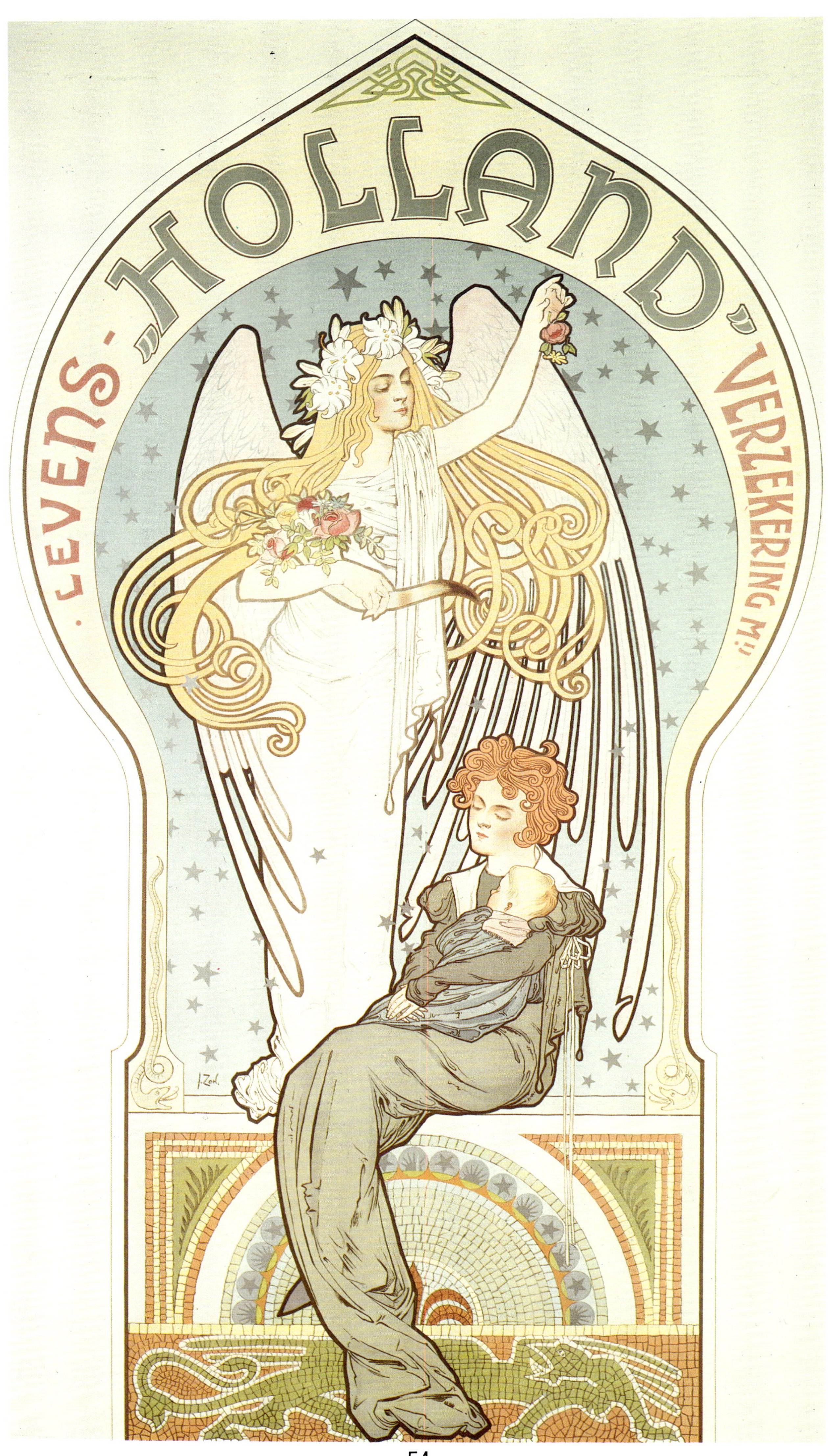
·LEVENS-„HOLLAND" VERZEKERING M!:

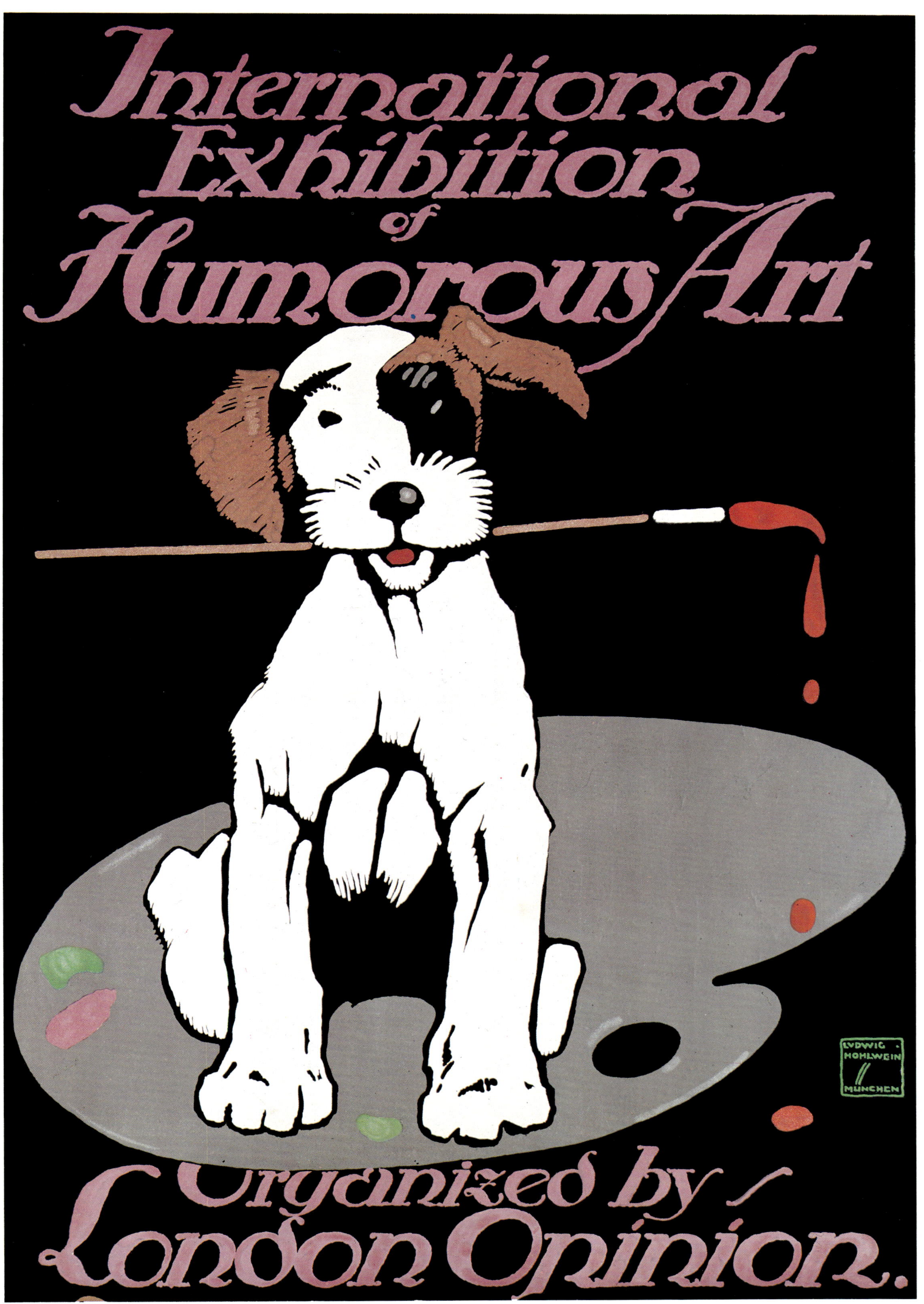
International
Exhibition
of
Humorous Art
LUDWIG HOHLWEIN MUNCHEN
Organized by
London Opinion.

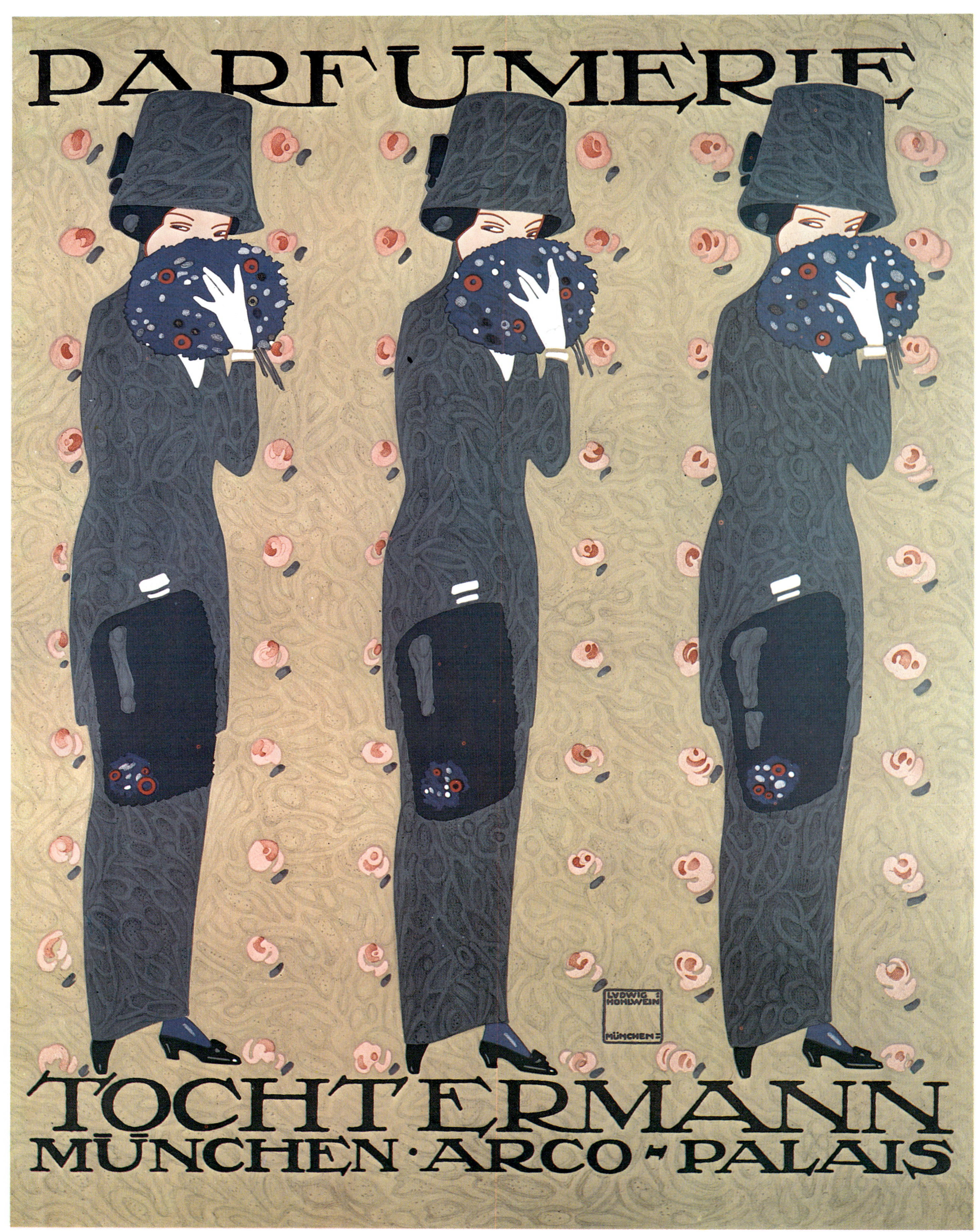
PARFUMERIE
LUDWIG HOHLWEIN
MÜNCHEN
TOCHTERMANN
MÜNCHEN · ARCO · PALAIS

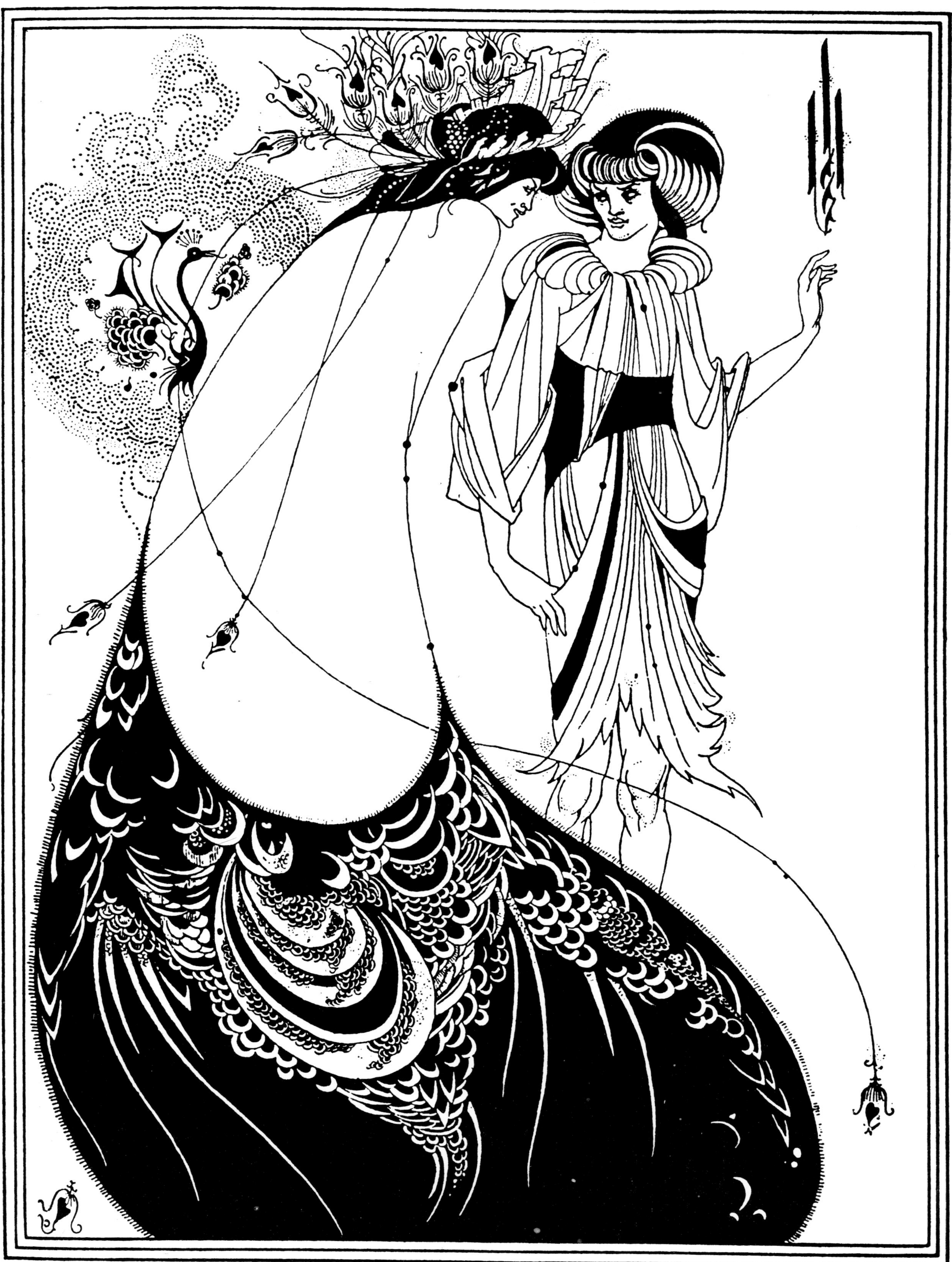

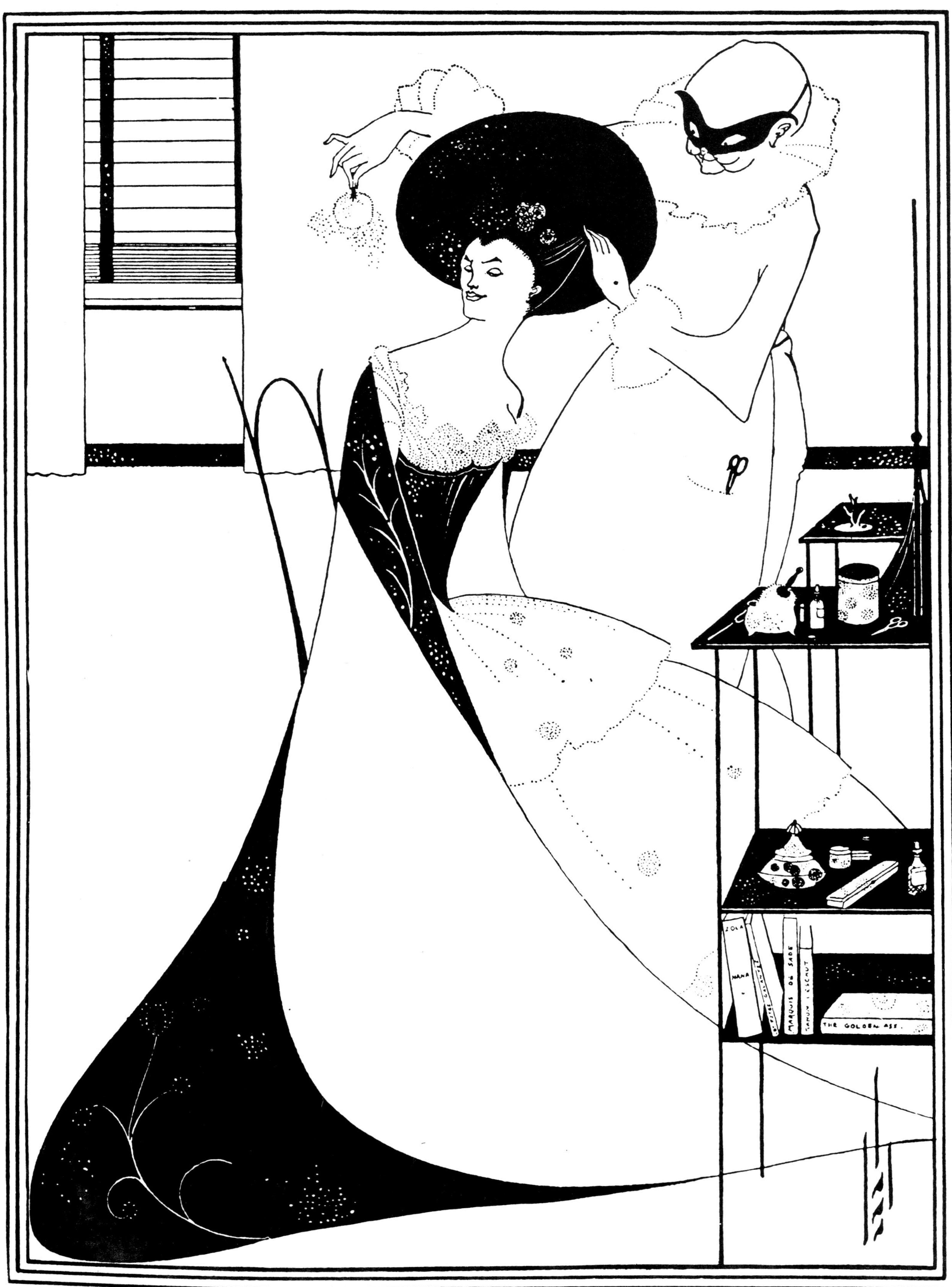
ZOLA
NANA
MARQUIS DE SADE
THE GOLDEN ASS.

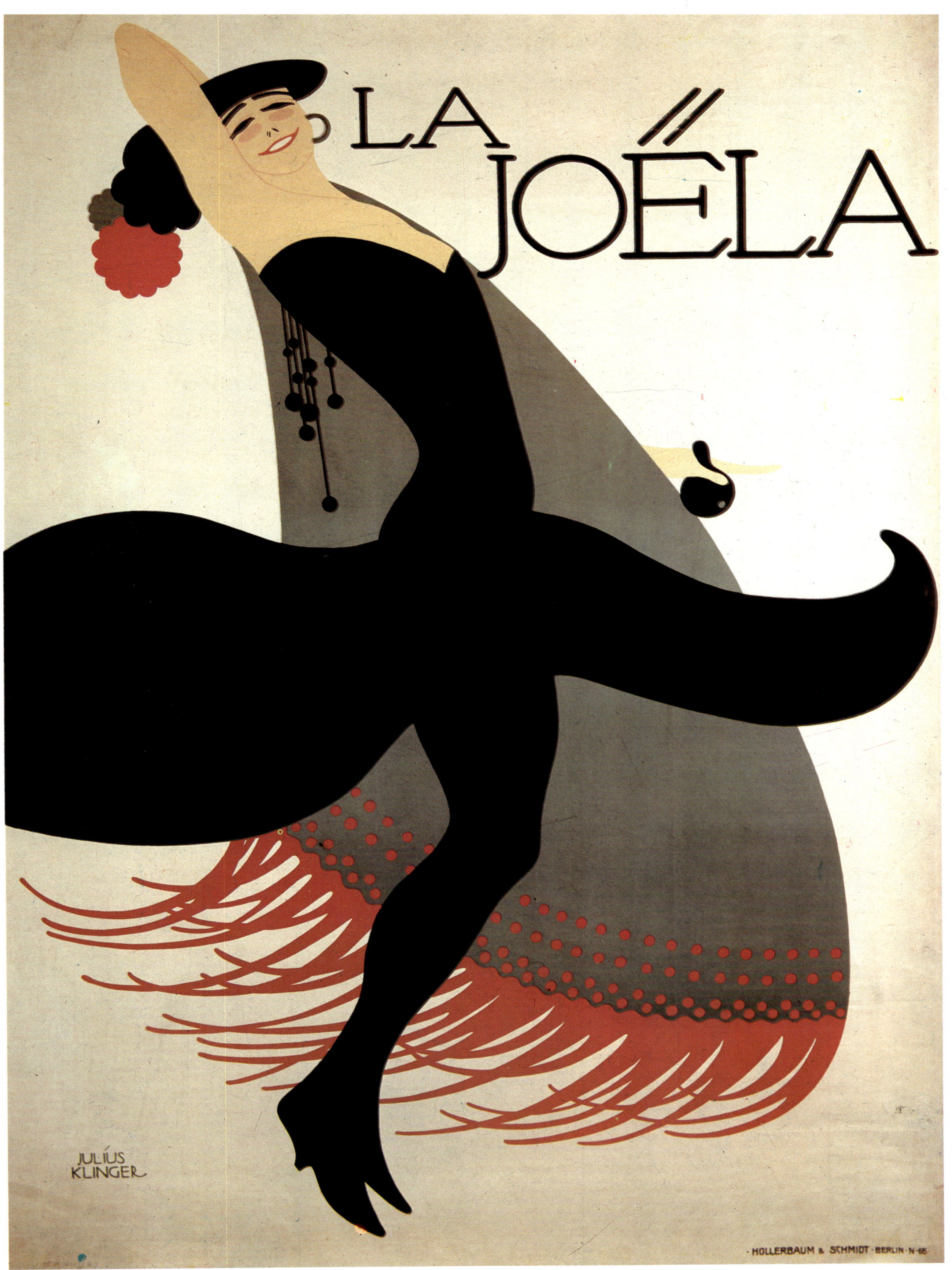
LA
JOÉLA
JULIUS
KLINGER
HOLLERBAUM & SCHMIDT · BERLIN · N · 65

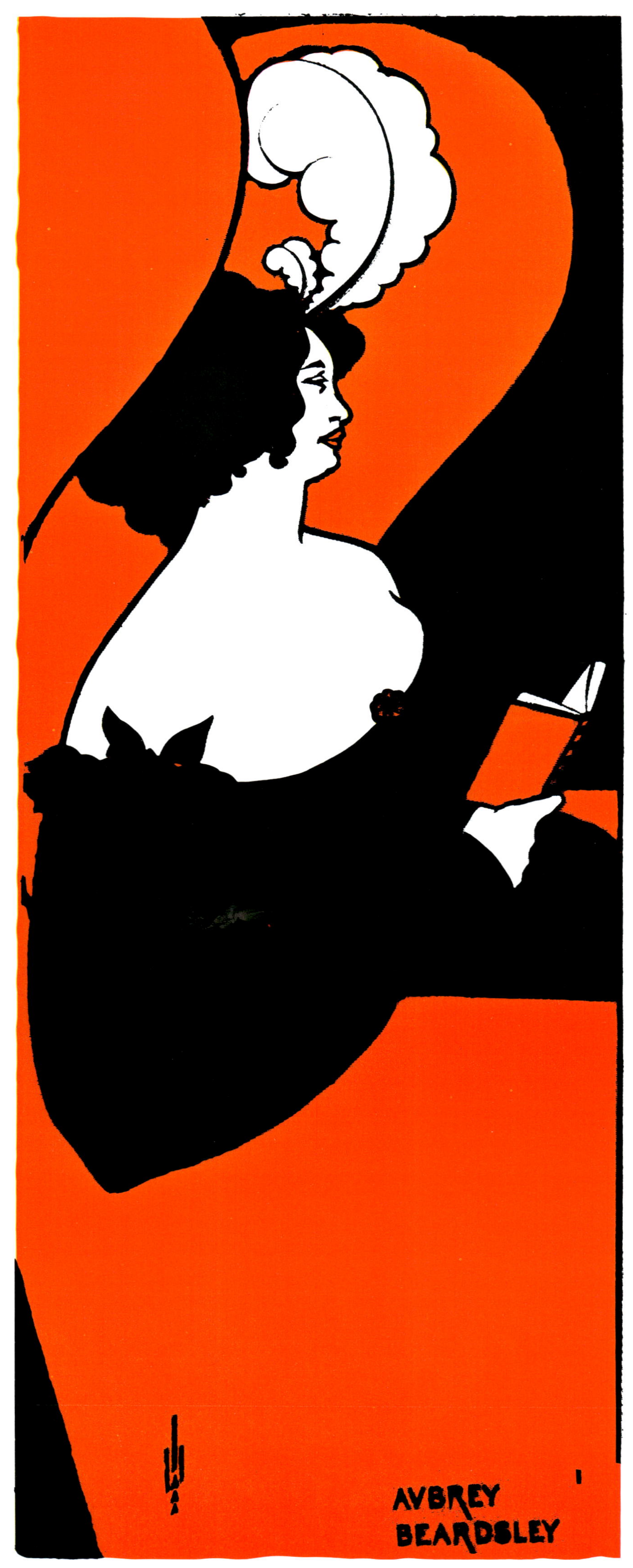
AVBREY
BEARDSLEY

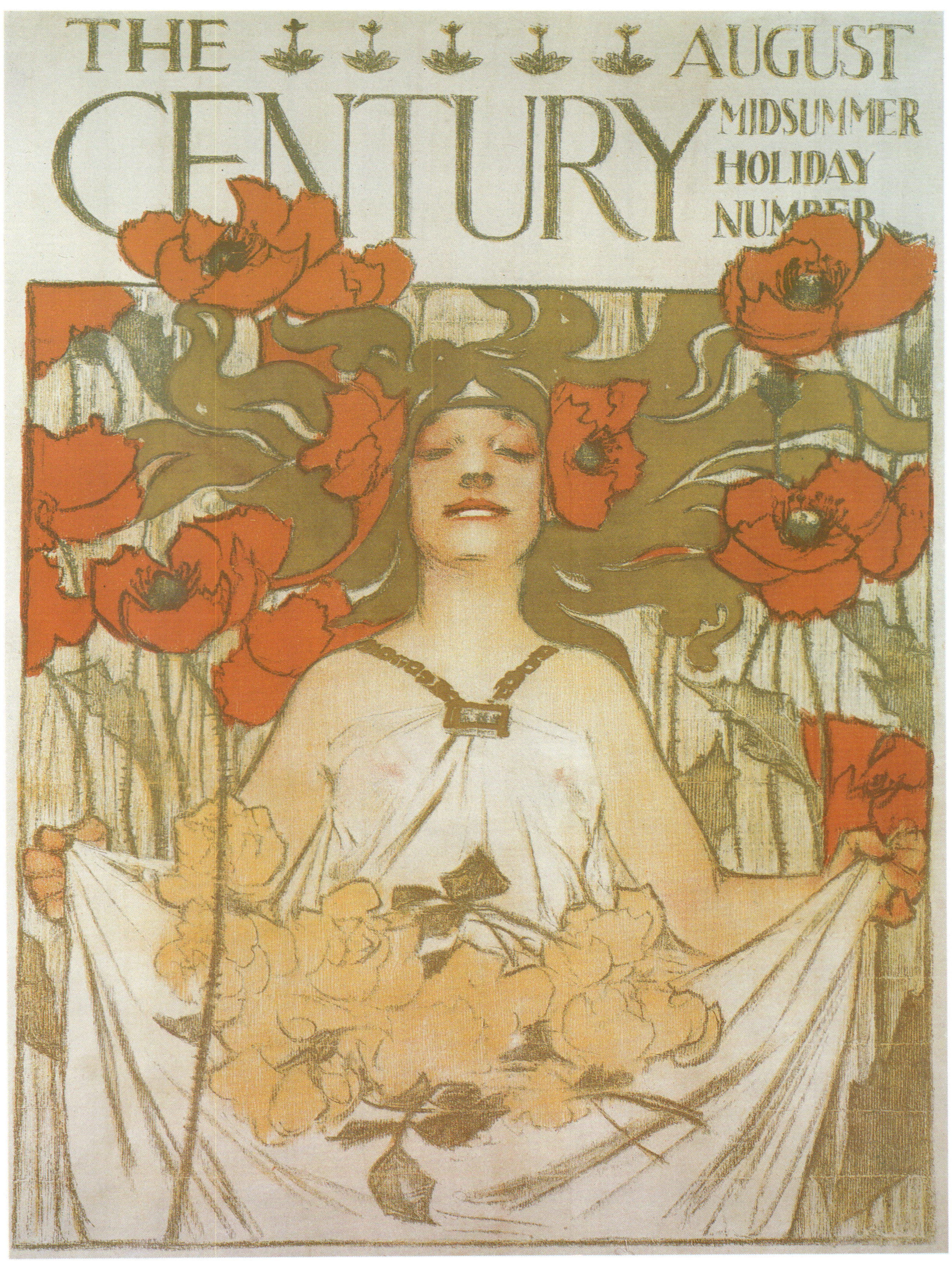
THE AUGUST
CENTURY
MIDSUMMER
HOLIDAY

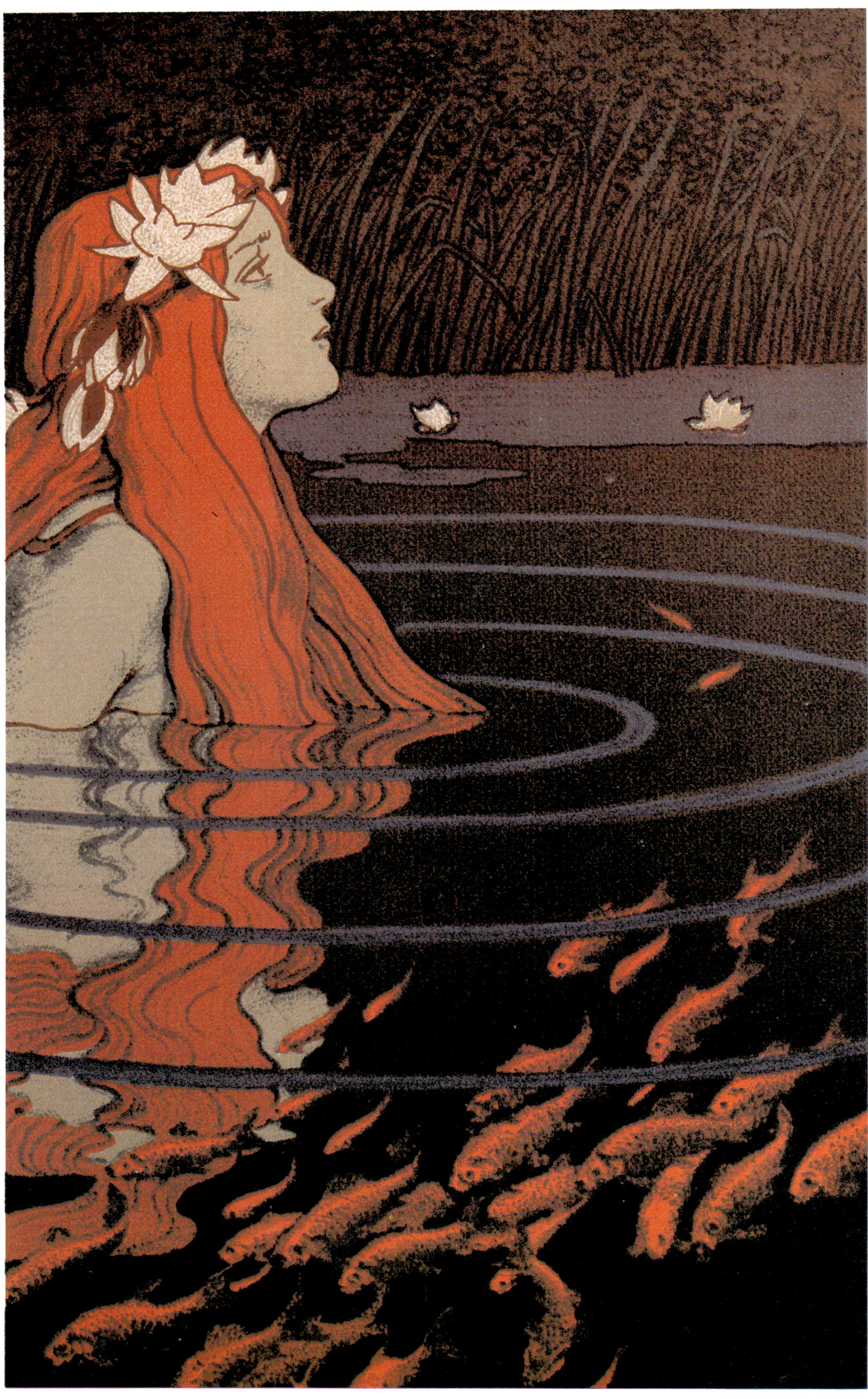

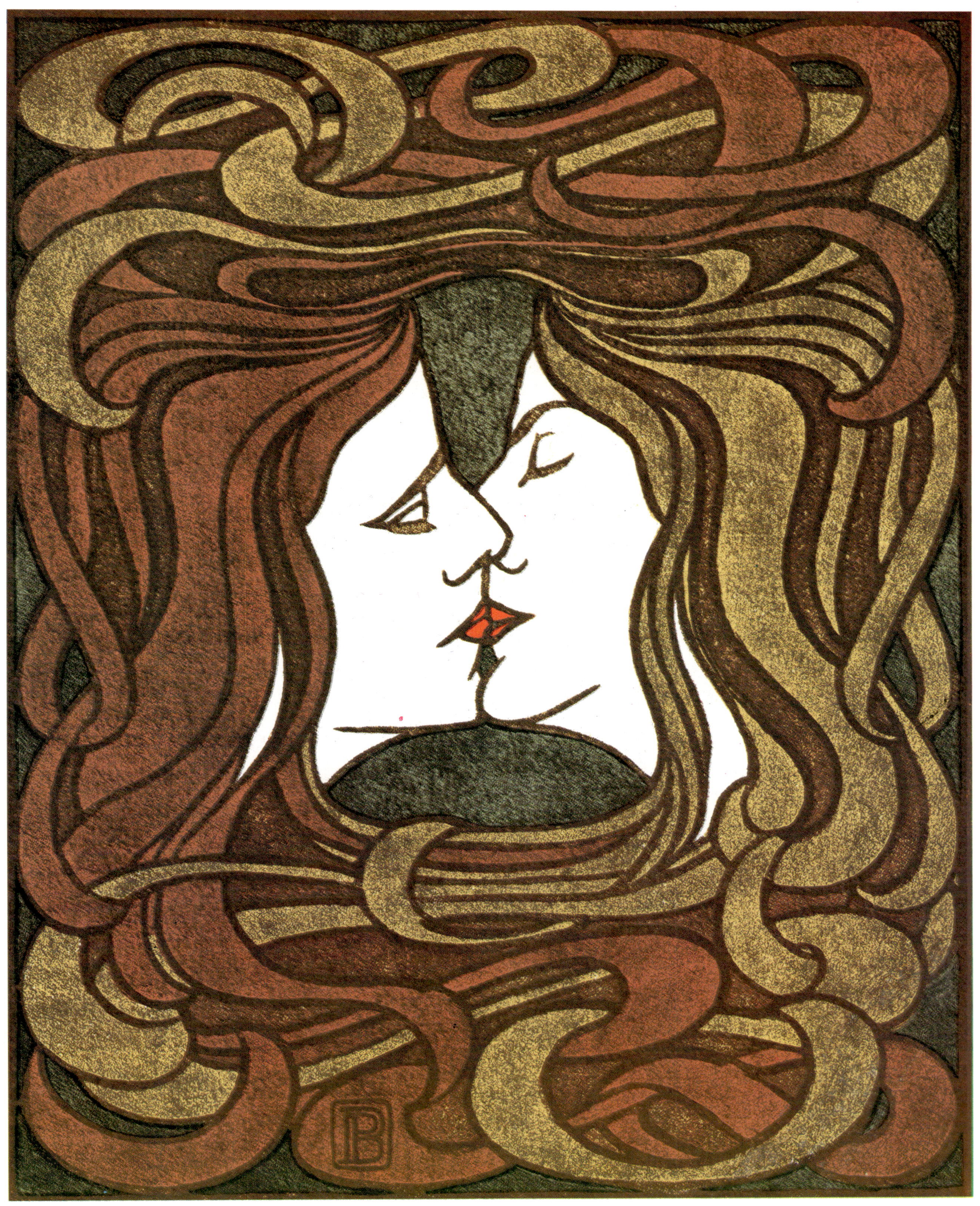

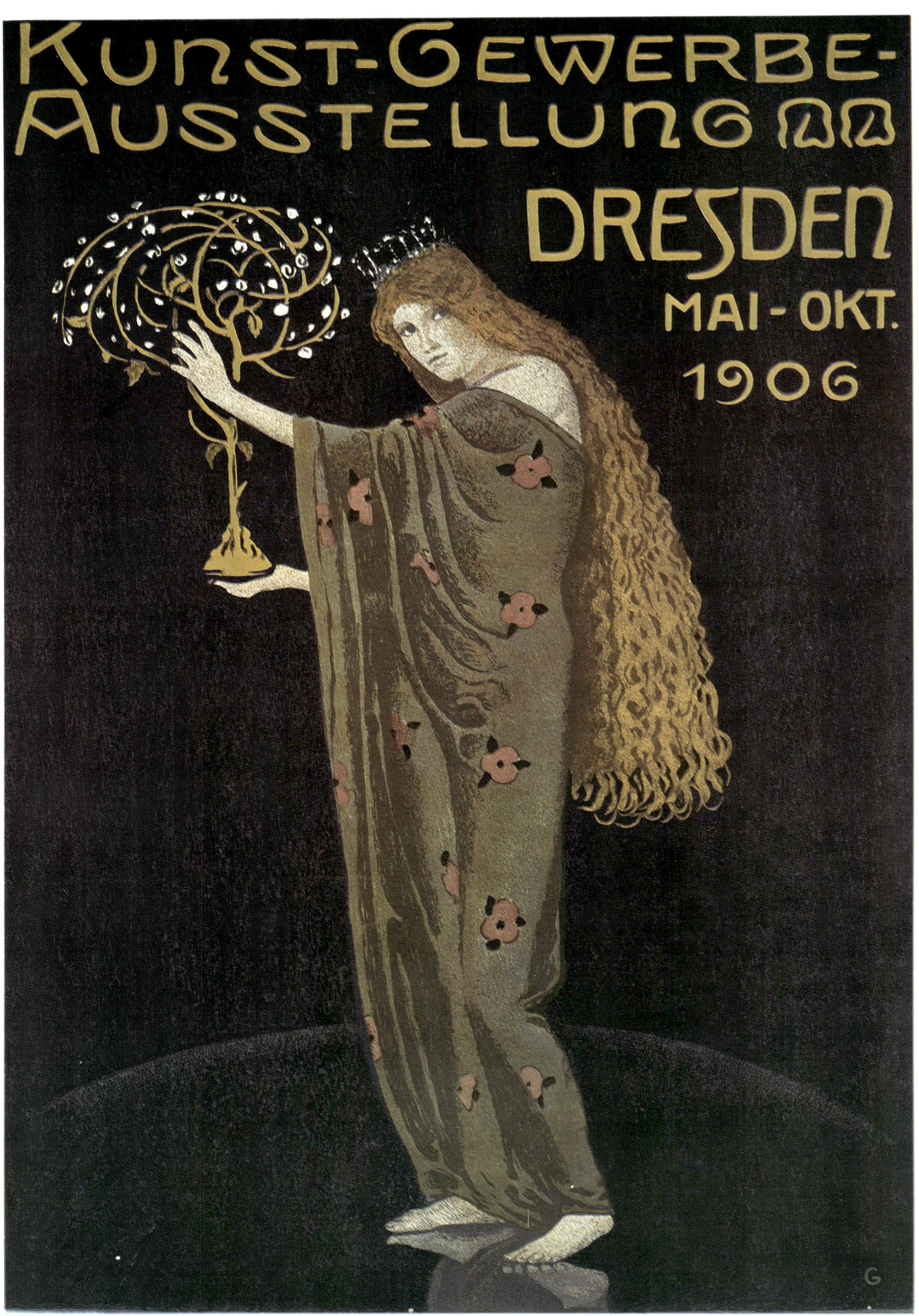
KUNST-GEWERBE-
AUSSTELLUNG
DRESDEN
MAI-OKT.
1906
G

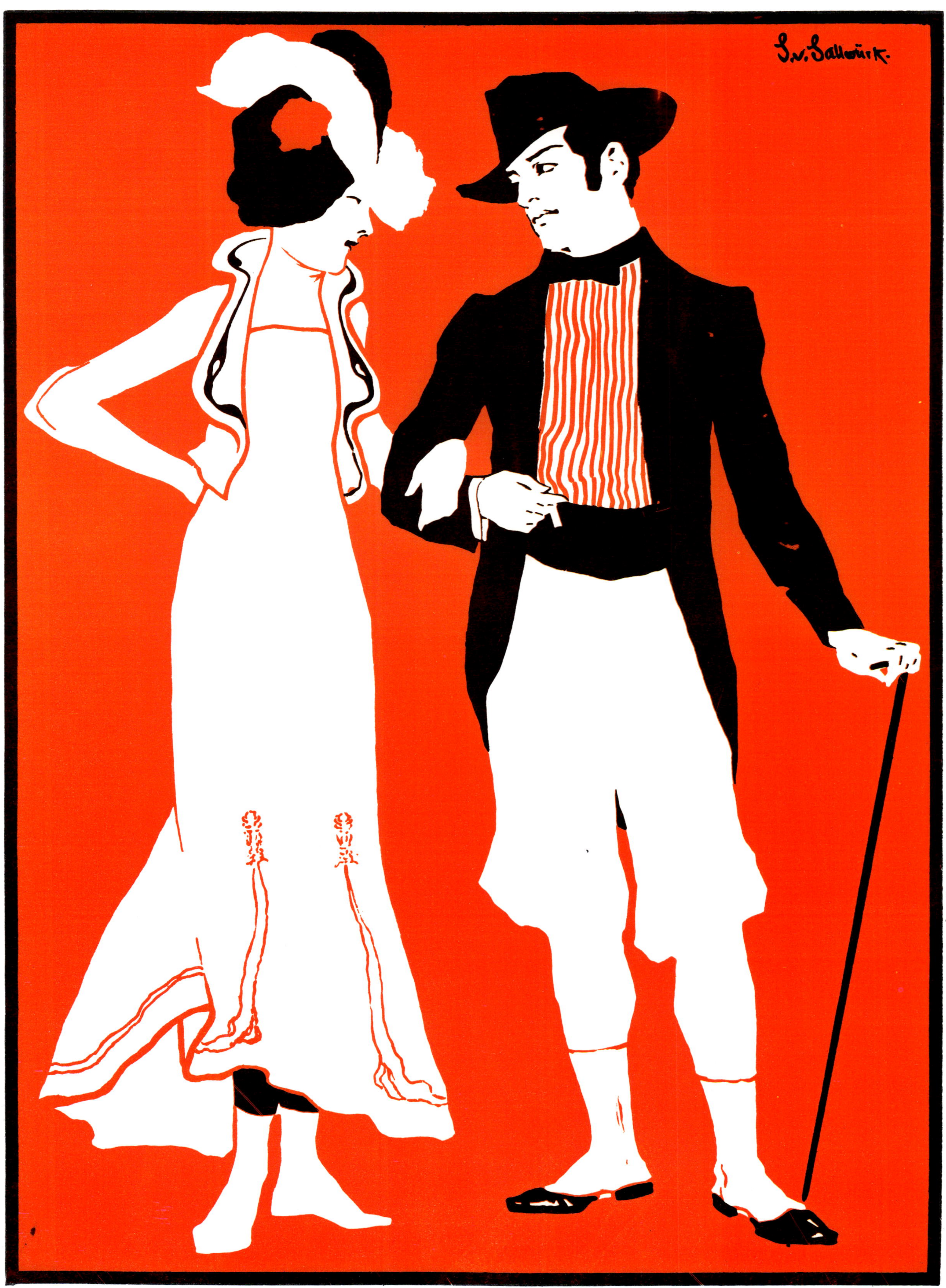
S.v.Sallwürk.

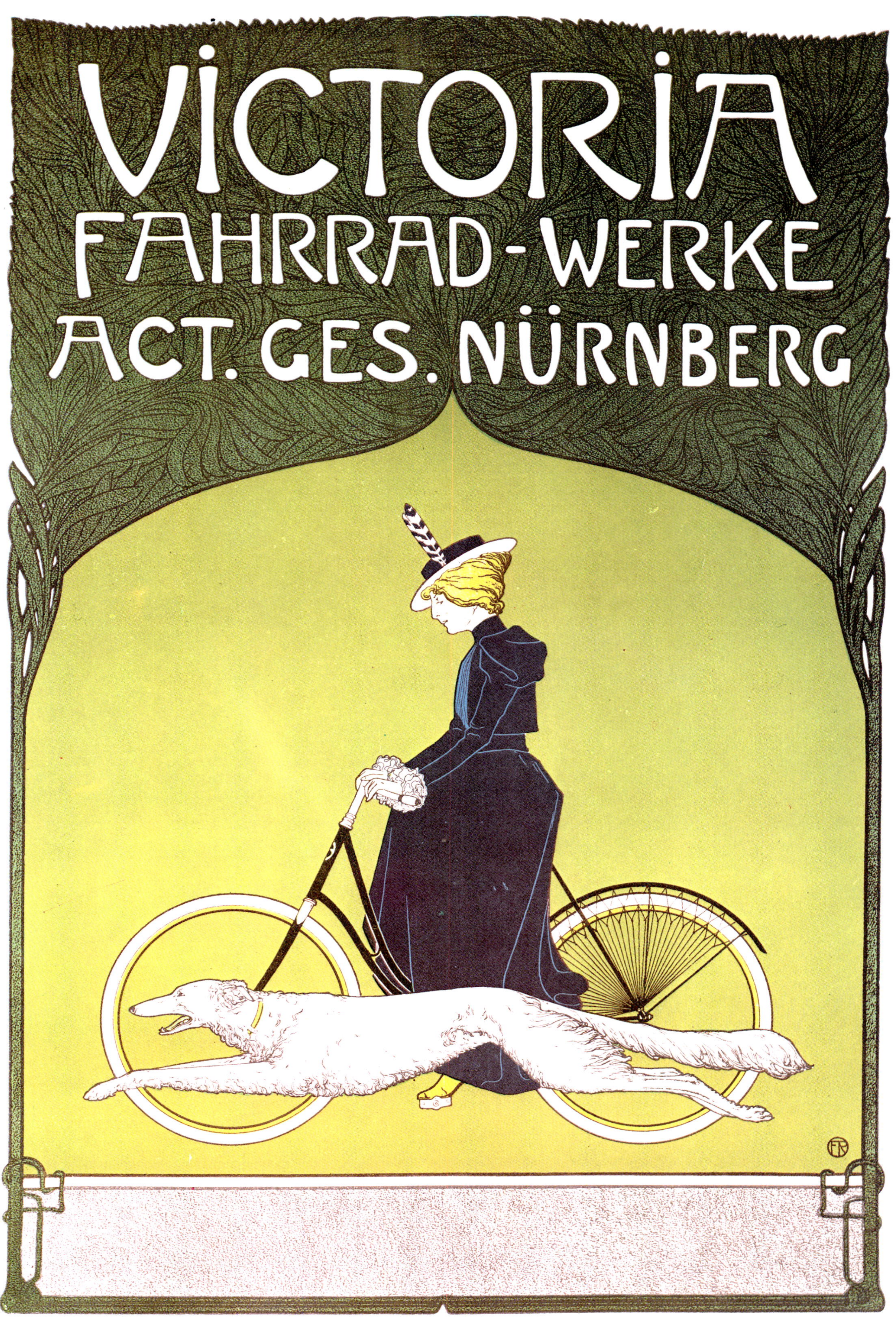
VICTORIA
FAHRRAD-WERKE
ACT. GES. NÜRNBERG

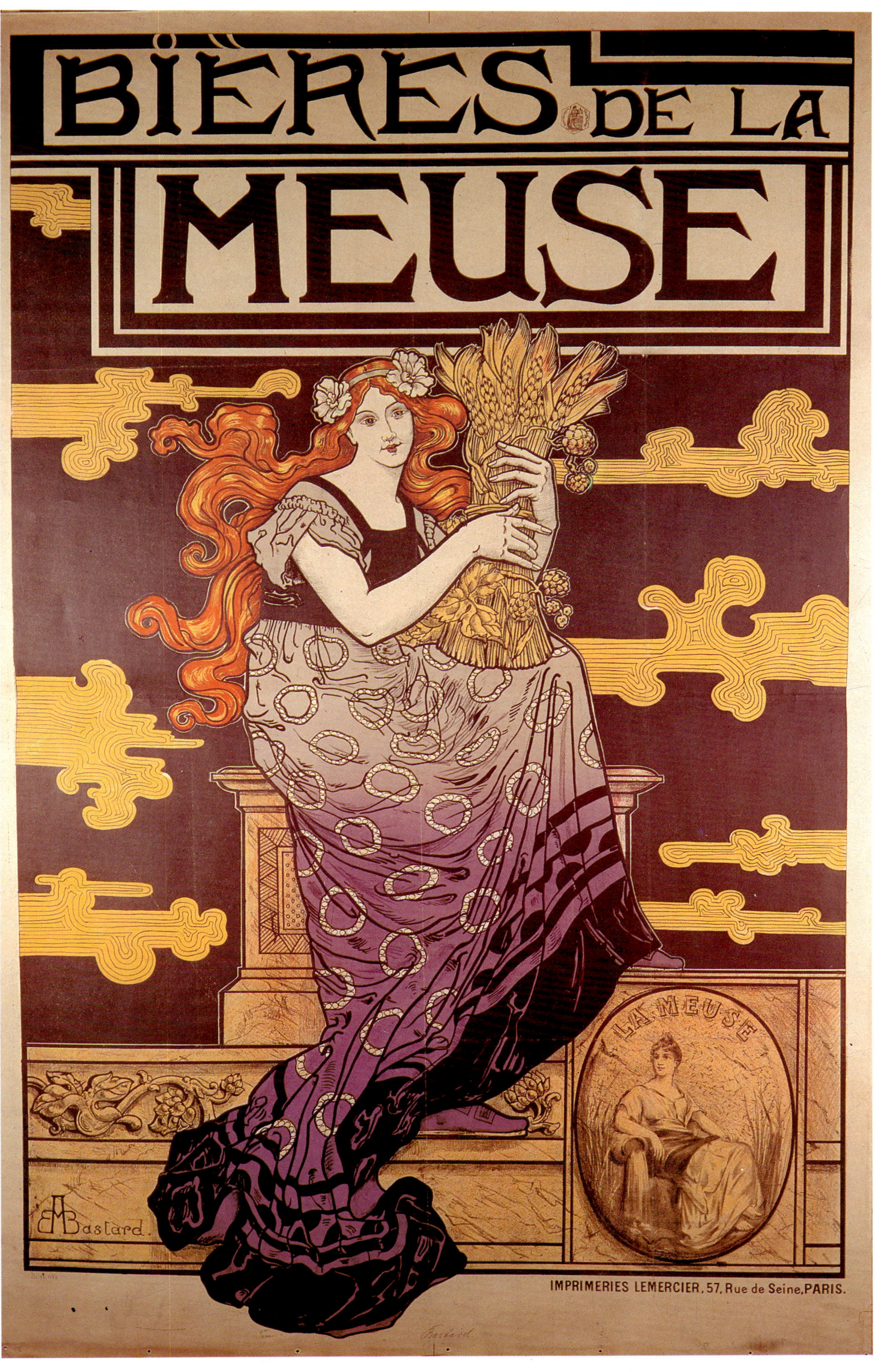
BIÈRES DE LA
MEUSE
LA MEUSE
Bastard.
IMPRIMERIES LEMERCIER, 57, Rue de Seine, PARIS.

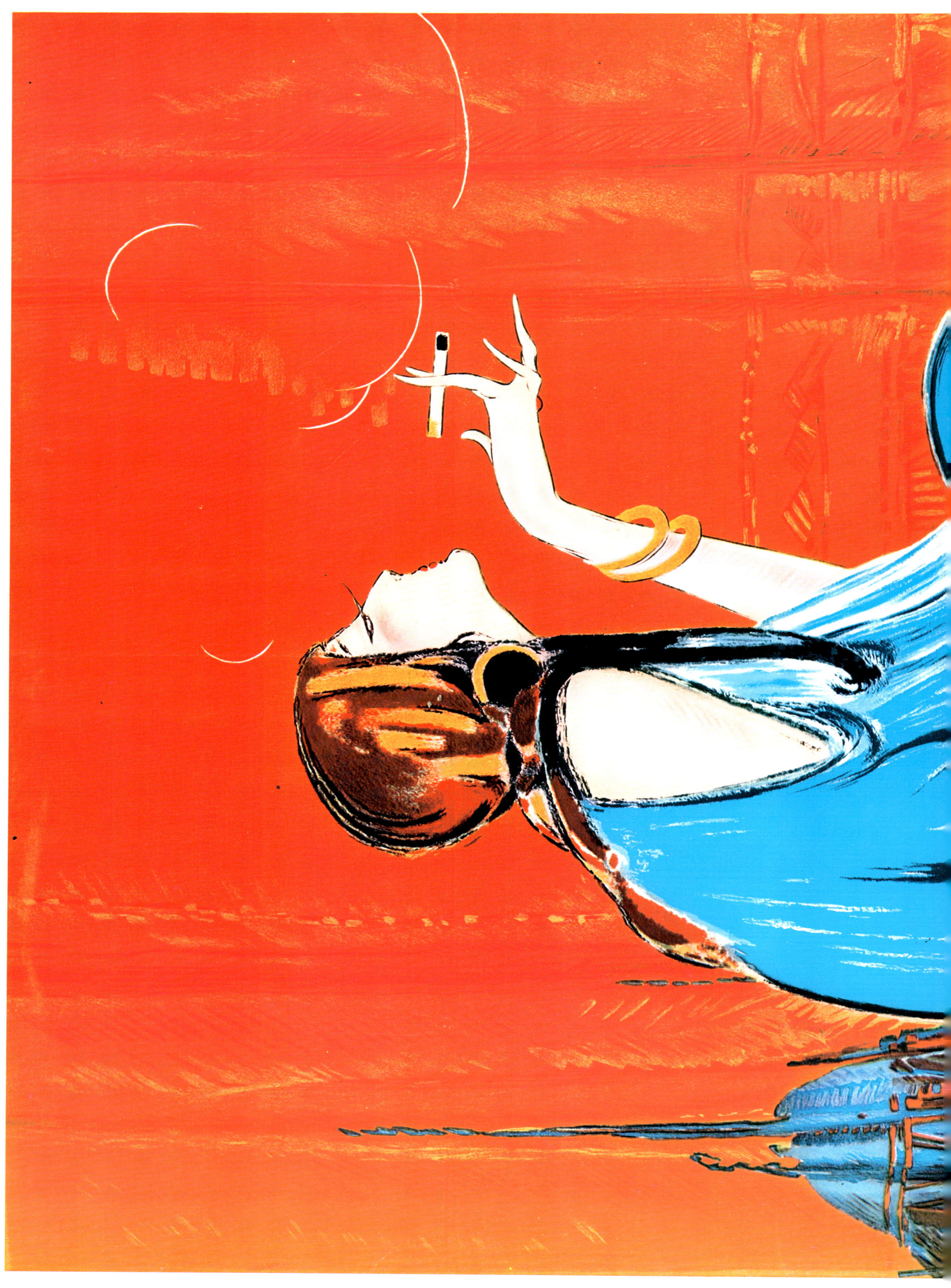

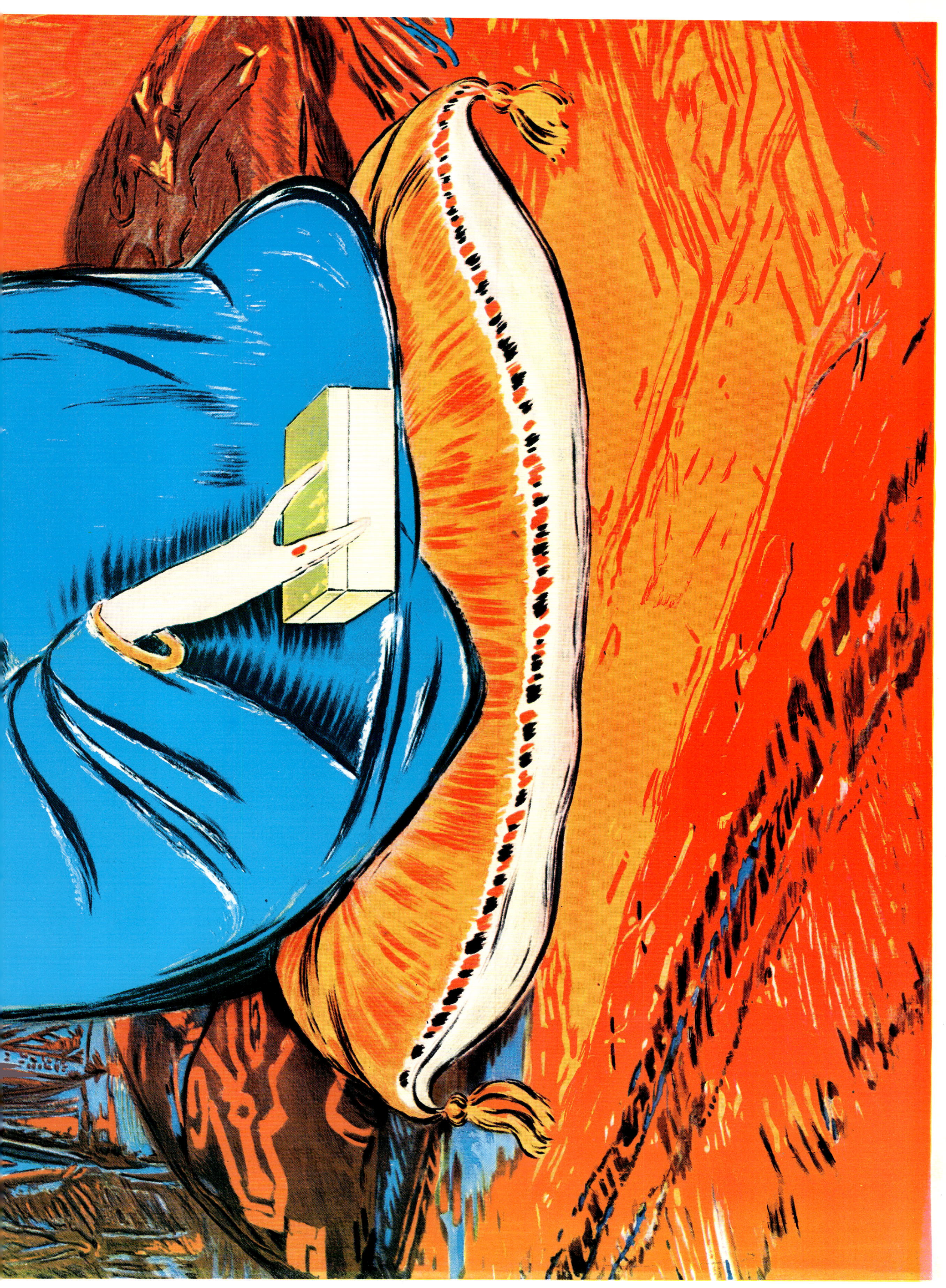

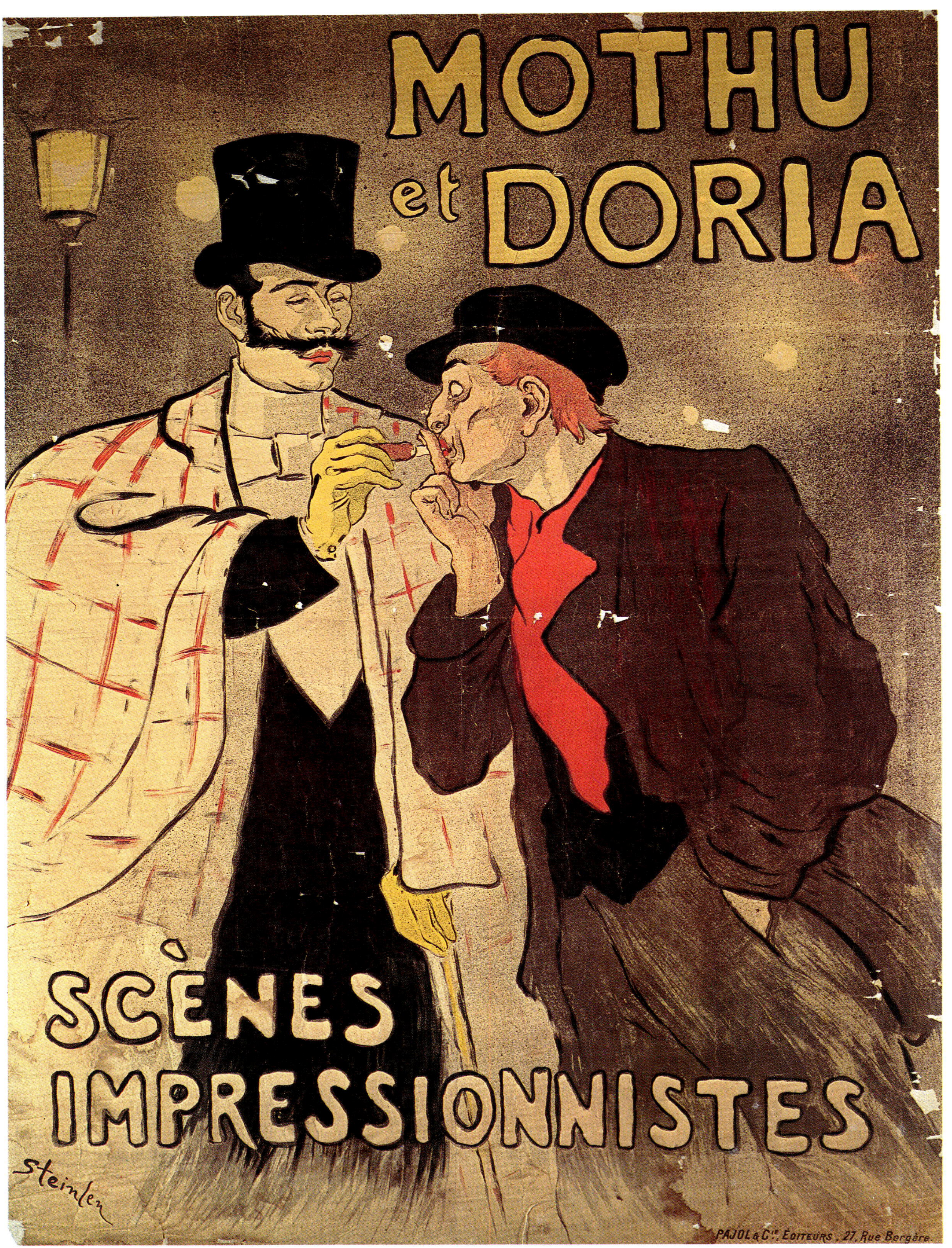
MOTHU
et DORIA
SCÈNES
IMPRESSIONNISTES
Steinlen
PAJOL & Cie, ÉDITEURS . 27, Rue Bergère.

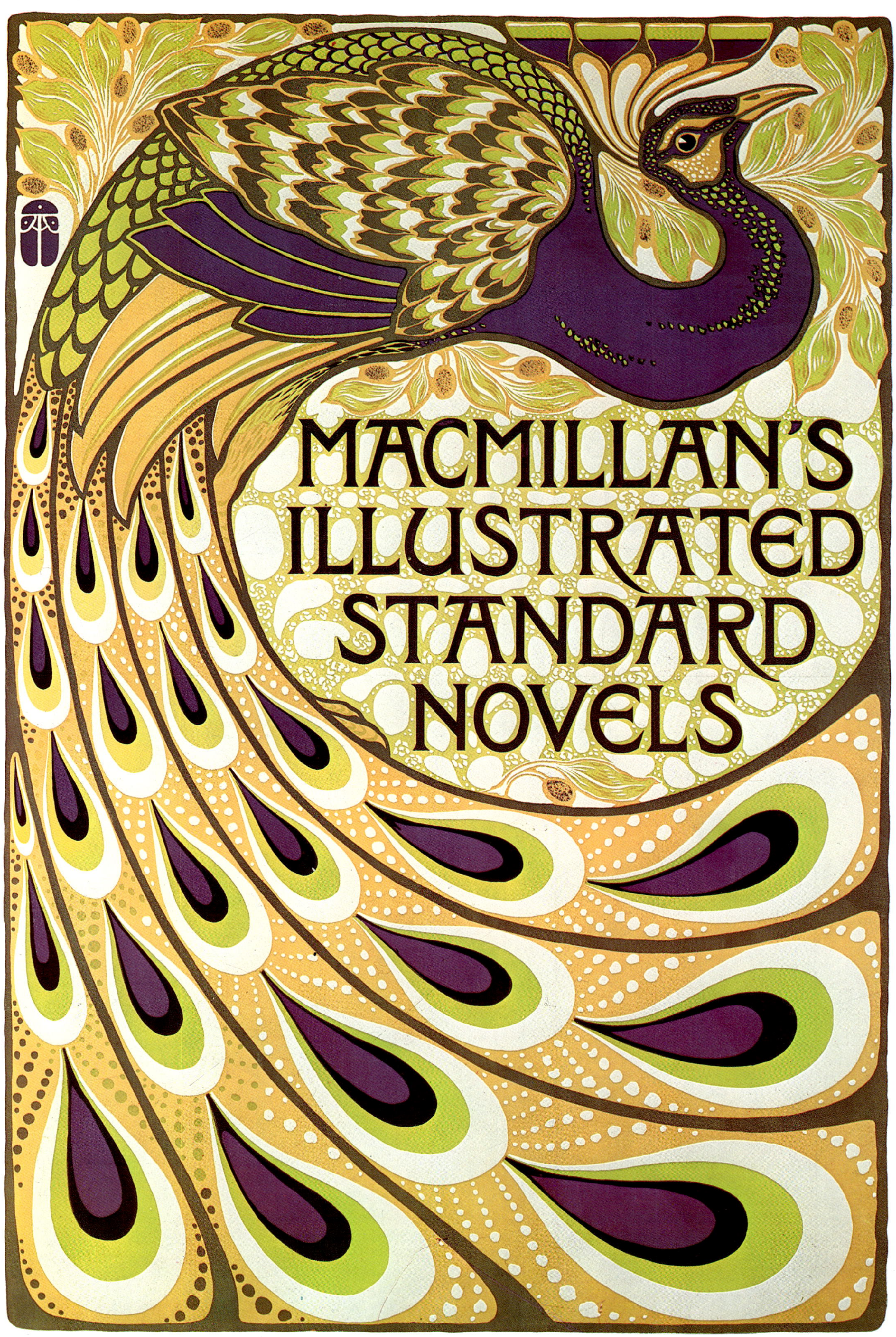
MACMILLAN'S
ILLUSTRATED
STANDARD
NOVELS

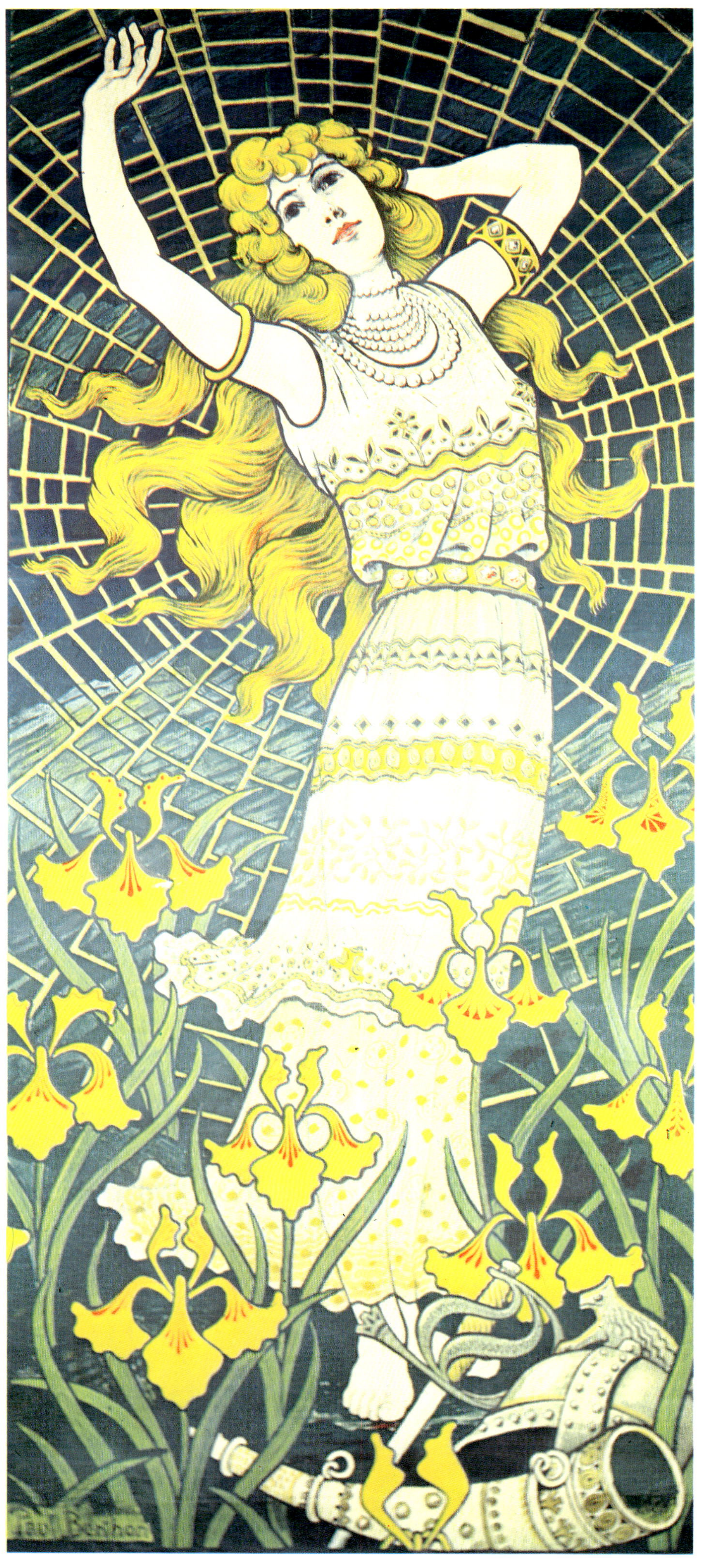
Paul Berthon

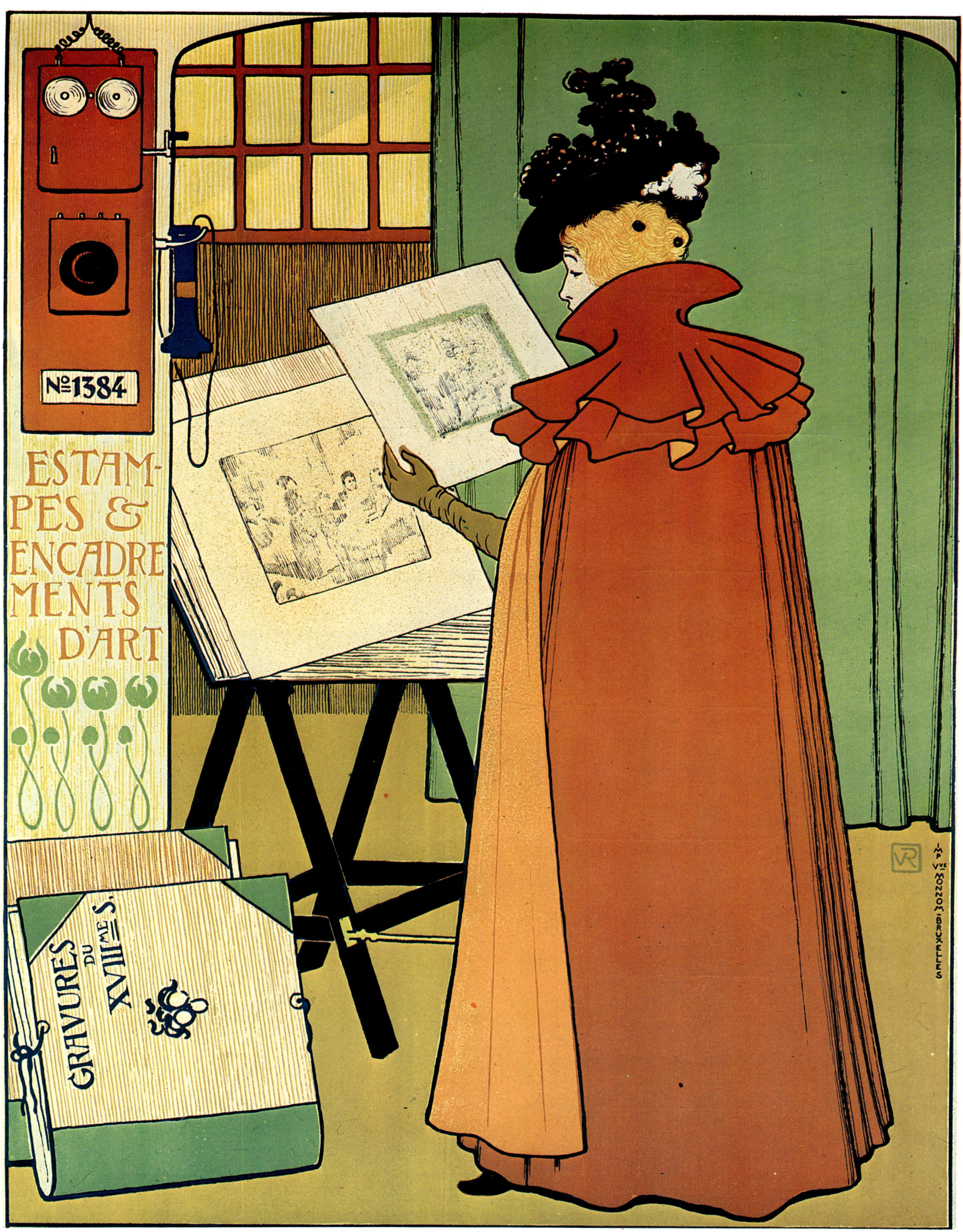

No 1384
ESTAMPES & ENCADREMENTS D'ART
GRAVURES DU XVIIIme S.
VR
IMP Vve MONNOM BRUXELLES

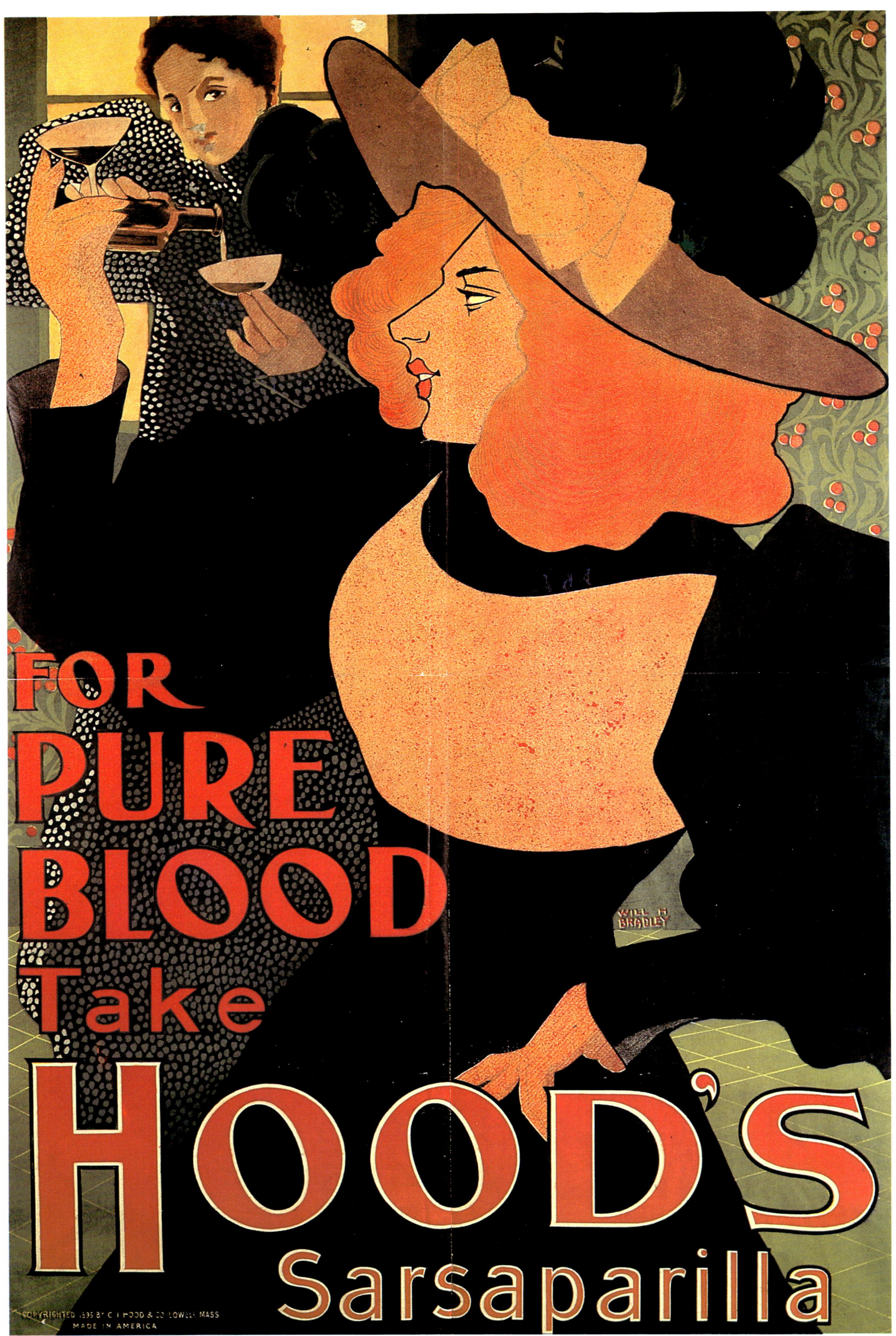
FOR
PURE
BLOOD
Take
HOOD'S
Sarsaparilla
WILL H BRADLEY
MADE IN AMERICA

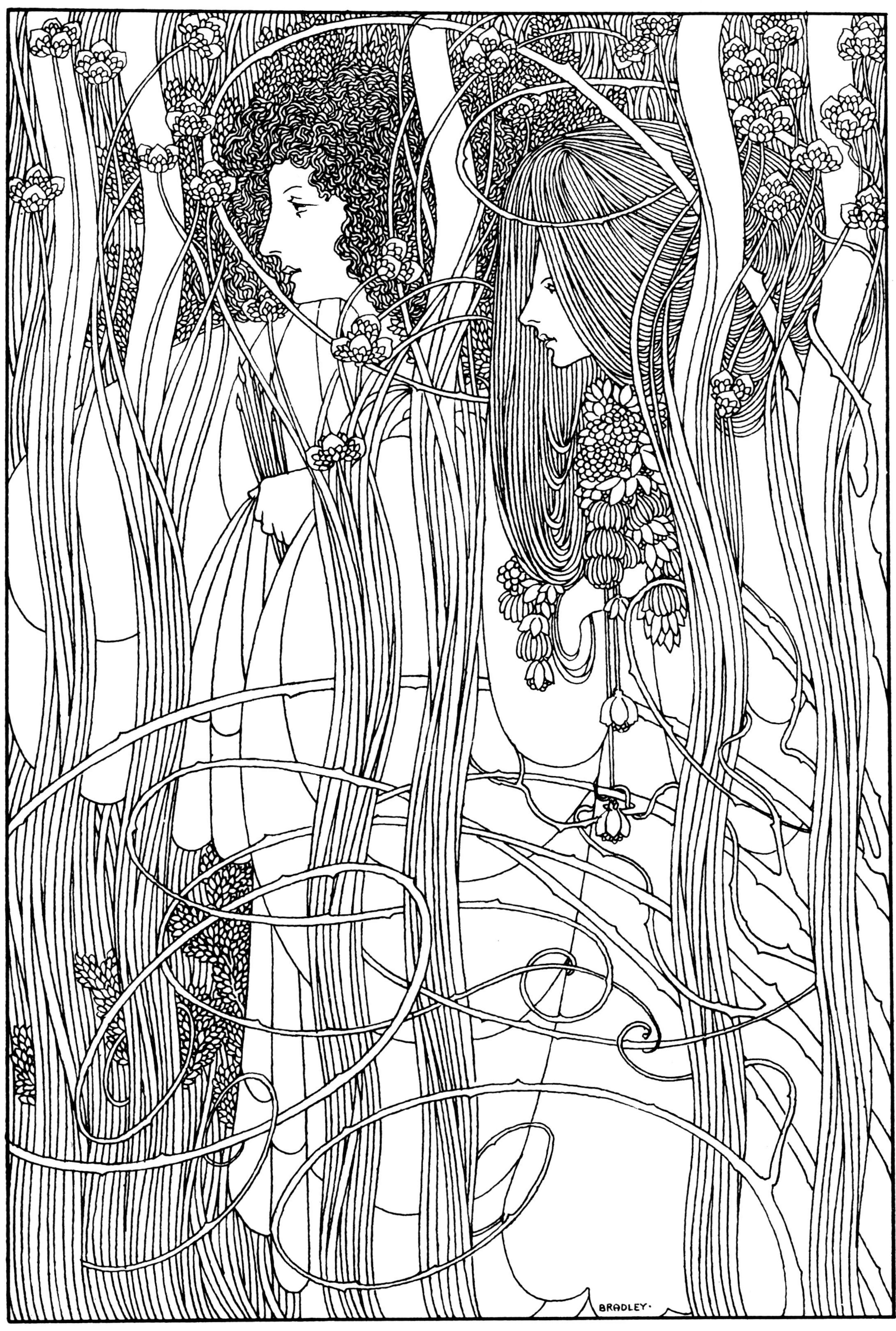
BRADLEY·

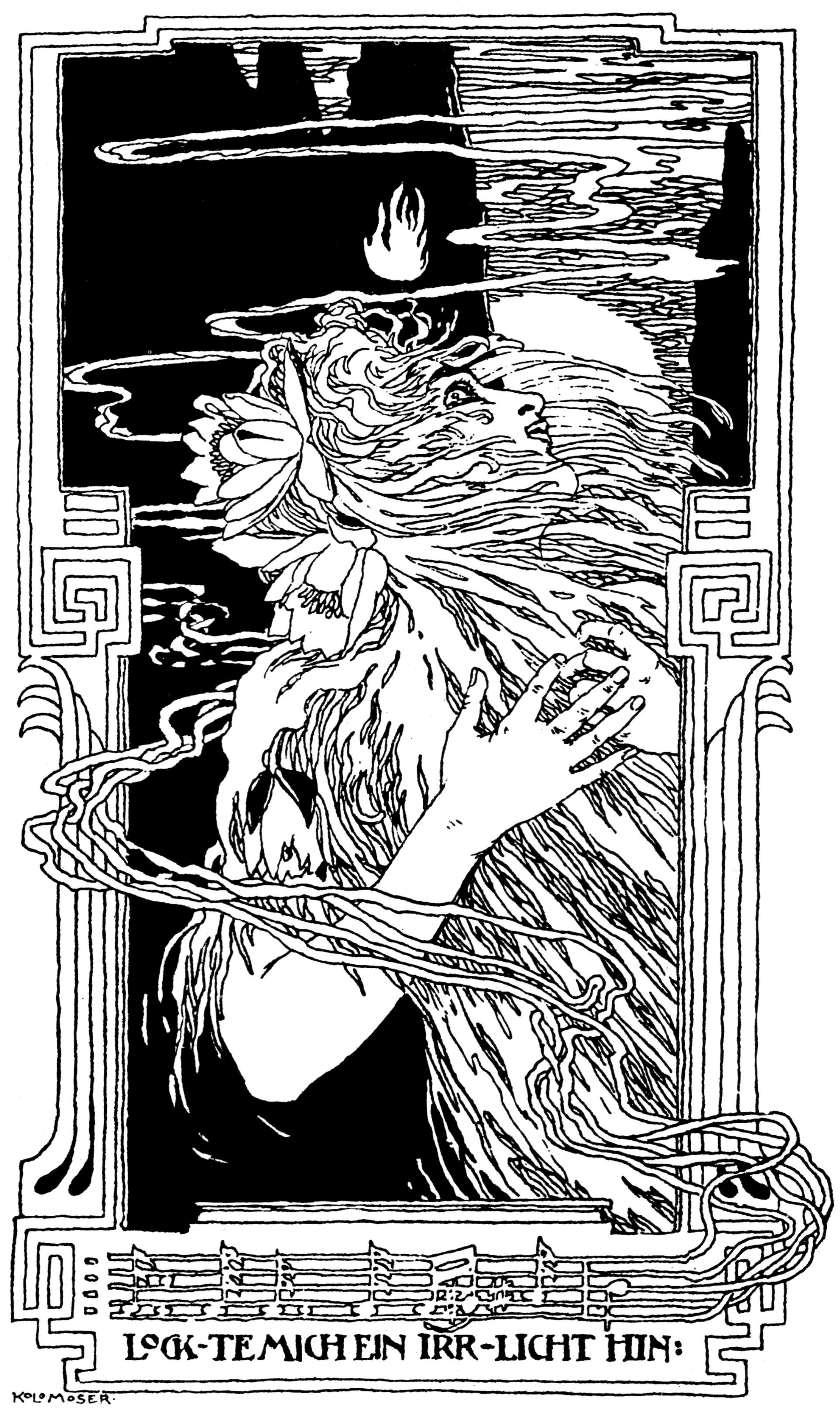
LOCK-TE MICH EIN IRR-LICHT HIN:
KOLO MOSER

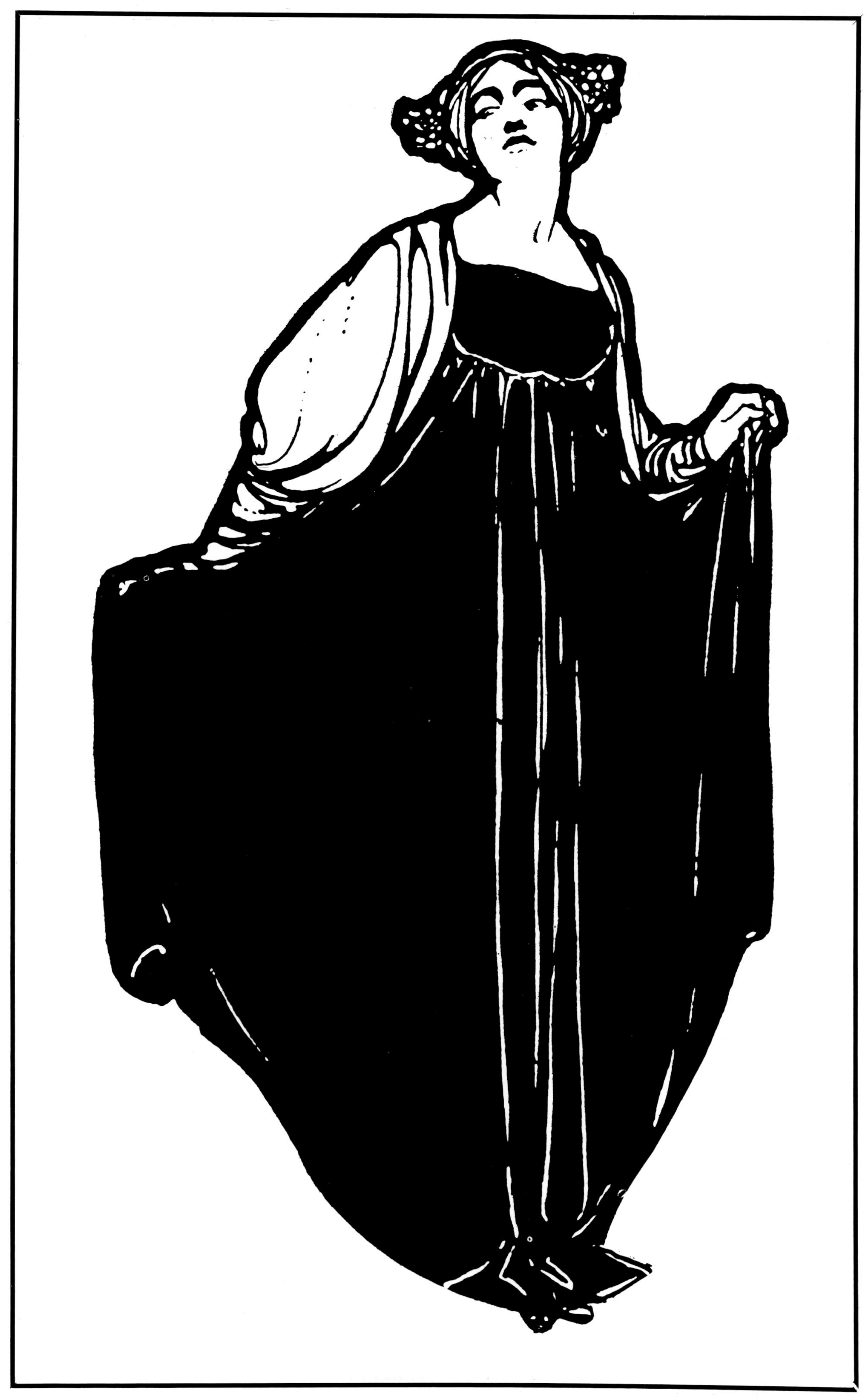

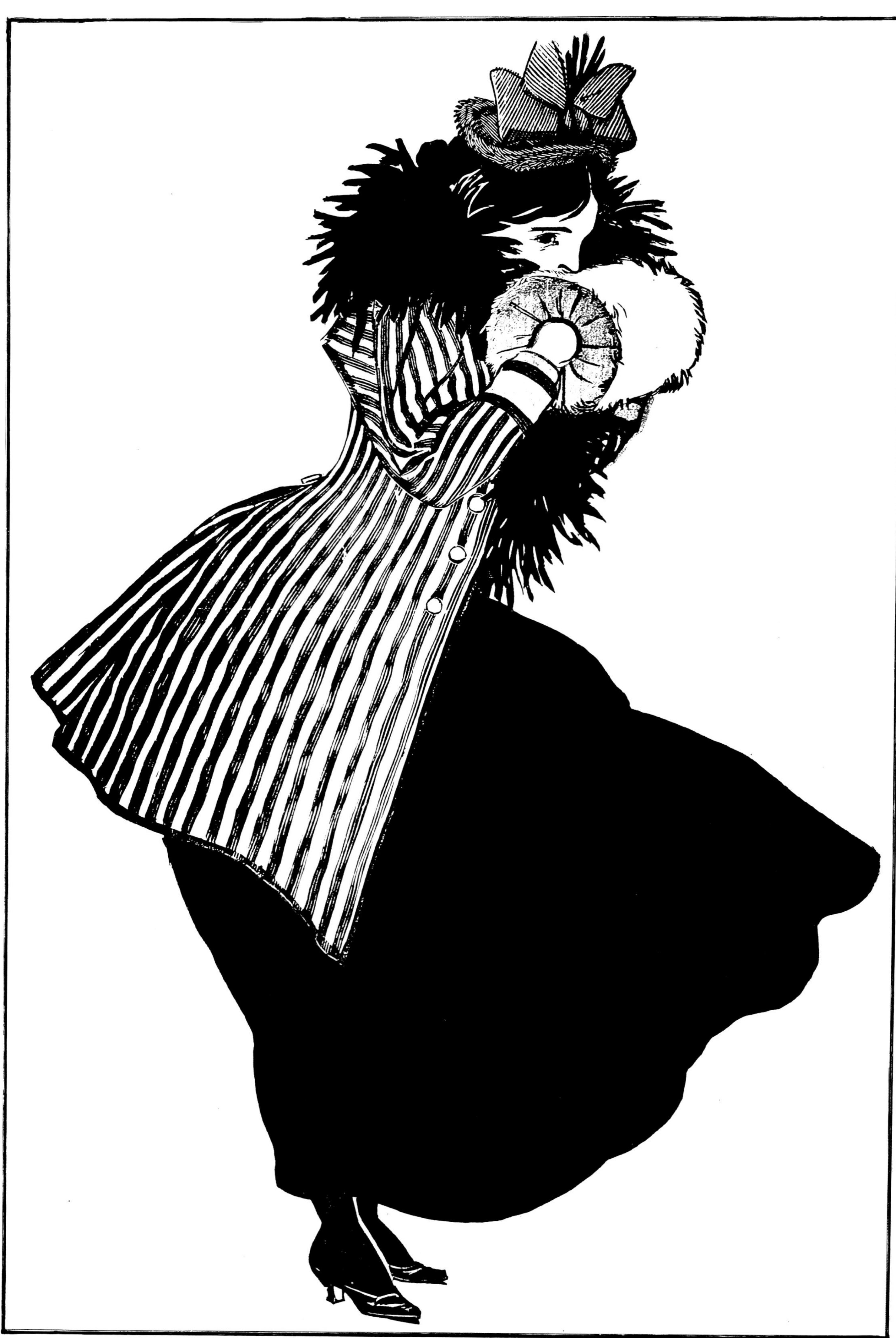

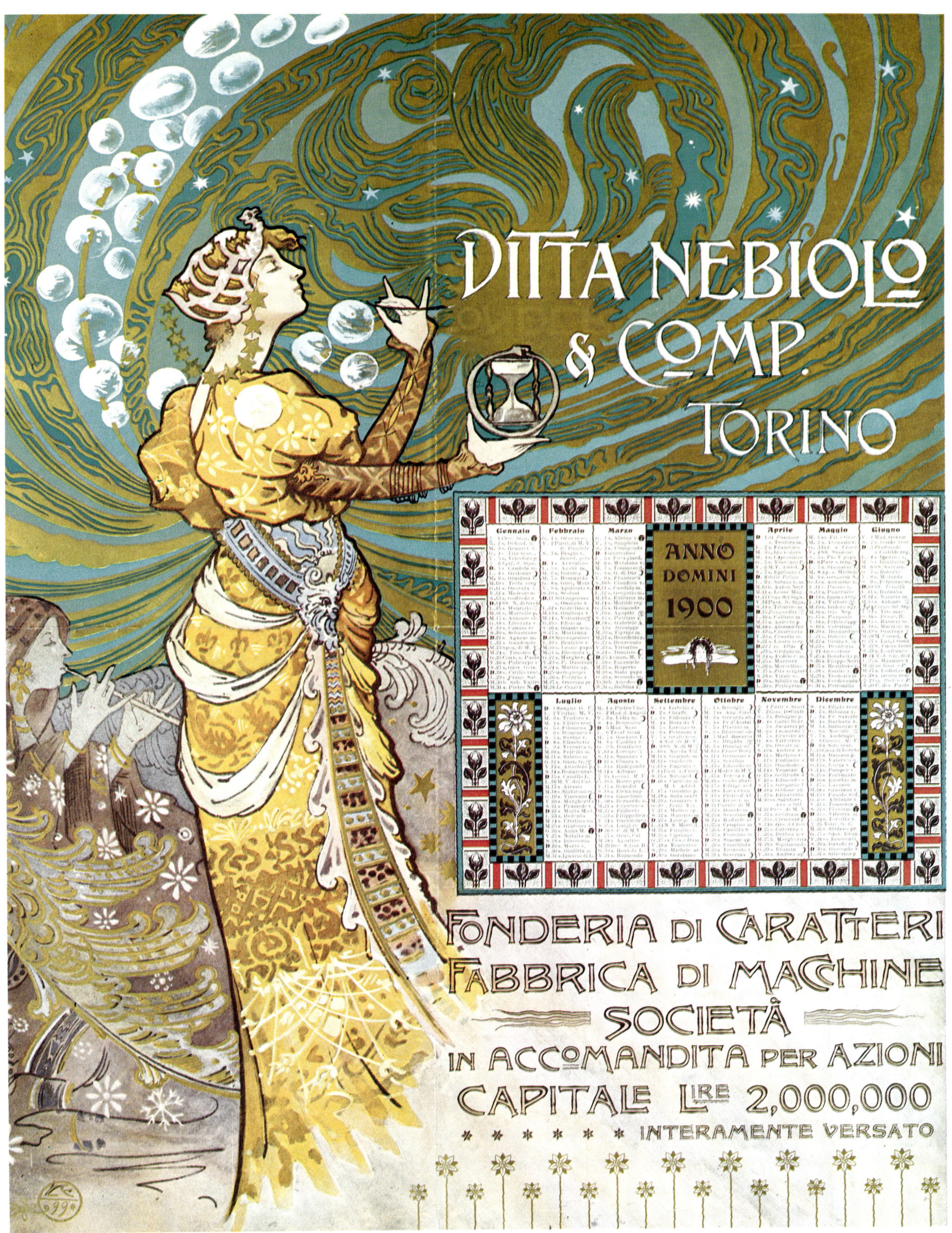
DITTA NEBIOLO
& COMP.
TORINO
Gennaio
Febbraio
Marzo
ANNO
DOMINI
1900
Aprile
Maggio
Giugno
Luglio
Agosto
Settembre
Ottobre
Novembre
Dicembre
FONDERIA DI CARATTERI
FABBRICA DI MACCHINE
SOCIETÀ
IN ACCOMANDITA PER AZIONI
CAPITALE LIRE 2,000,000
INTERAMENTE VERSATO

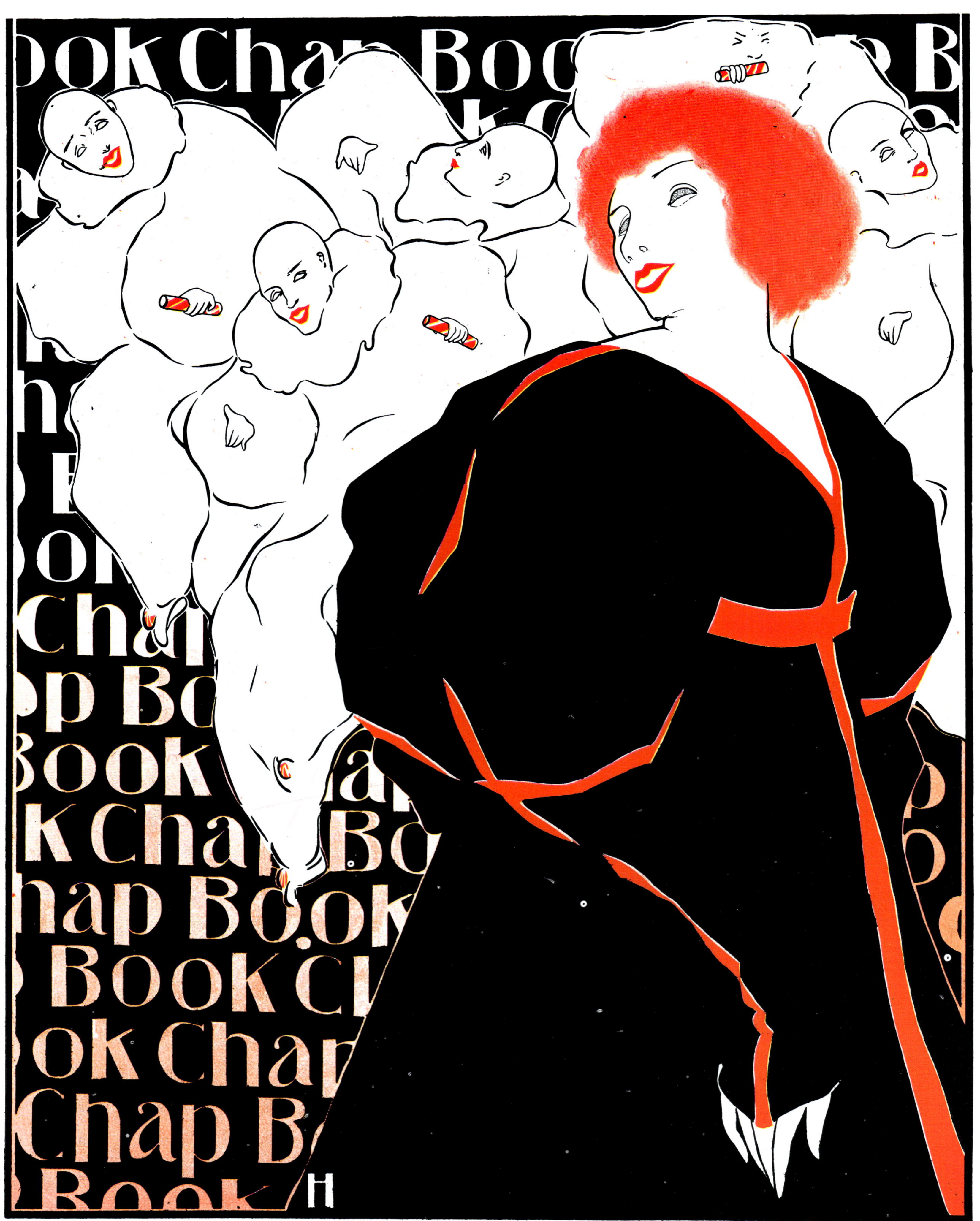
ook Chap Boo
Chap
p Bo
Book
k Chap Bo
hap Book
Book C
ok Chap
Chap B
Book
H

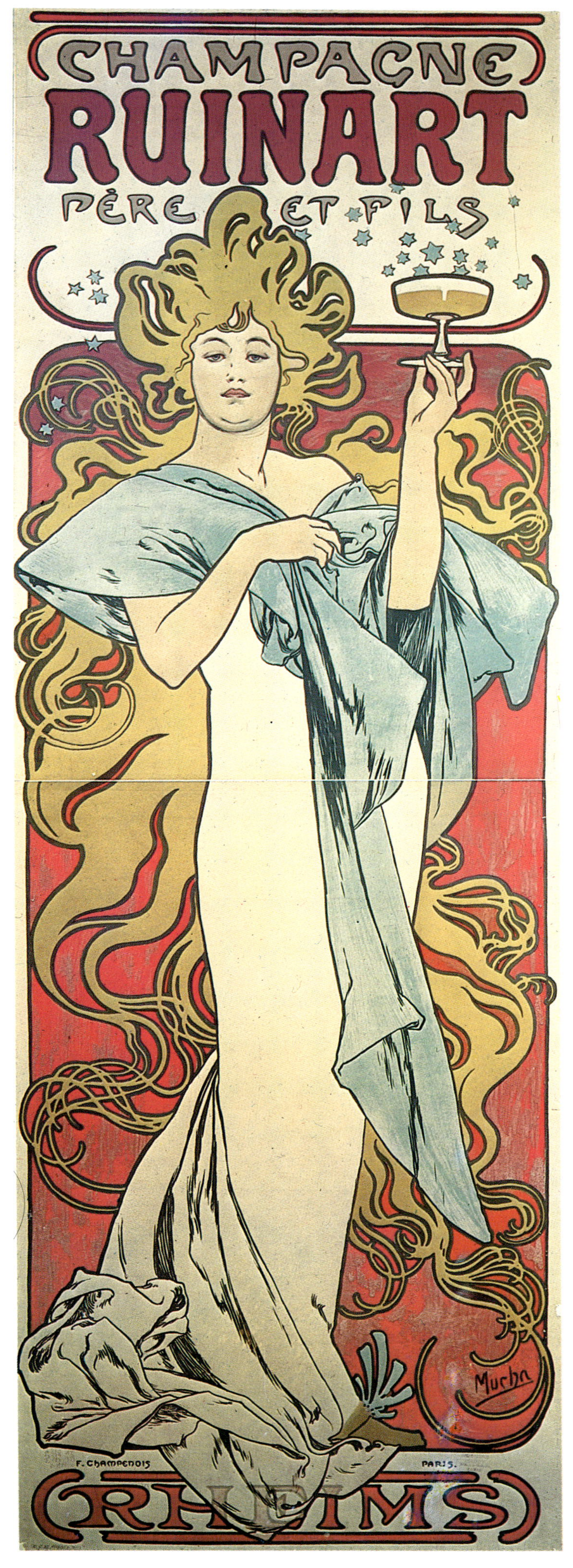
CHAMPAGNE
RUINART
PÈRE ET FILS
Mucha
F. CHAMPENOIS PARIS.
RHEIMS

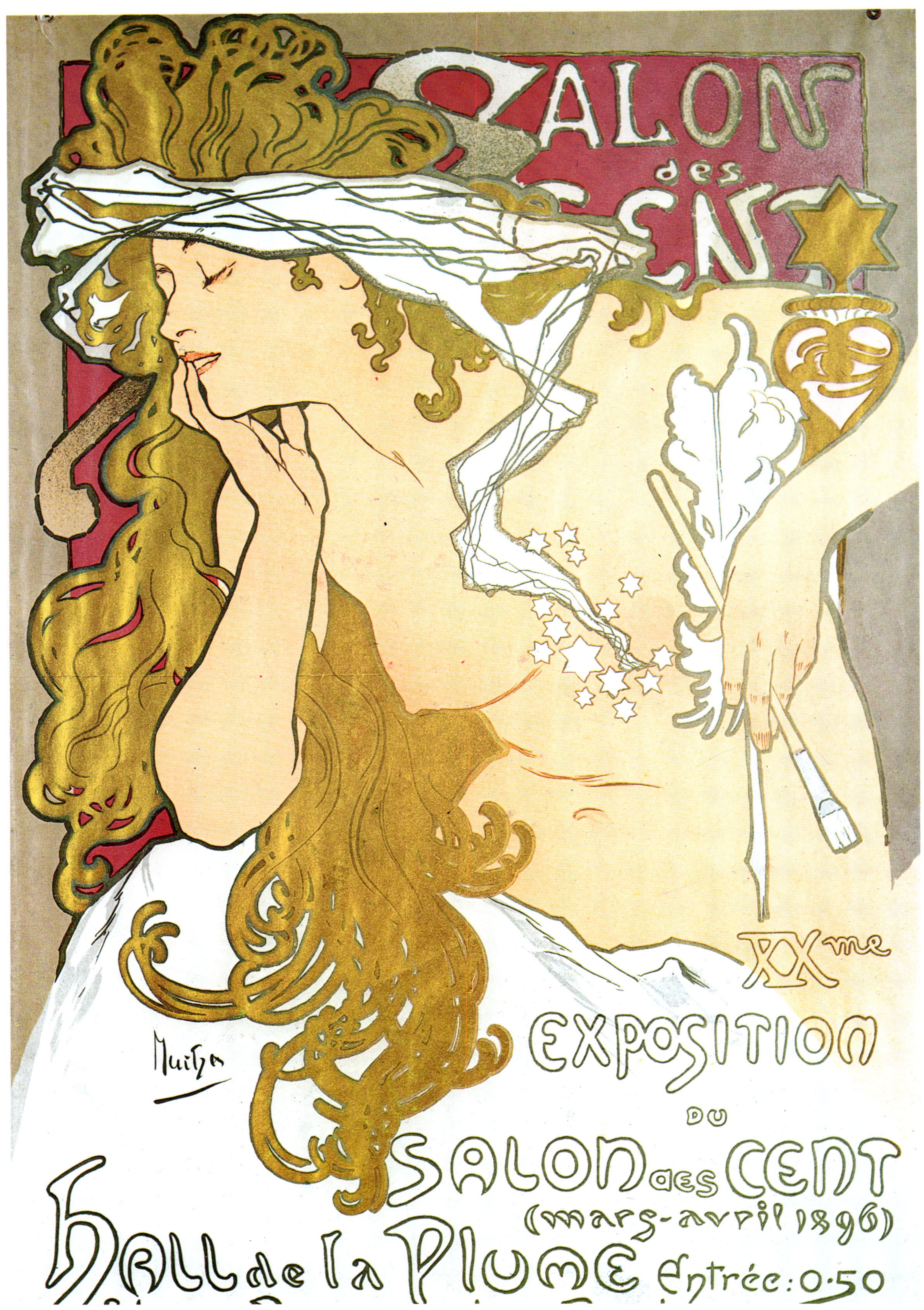
SALON des CENT
XXme
EXPOSITION
DU
SALON des CENT
(mars-avril 1896)
HALL de la PLUME
Entrée: 0·50
Mucha

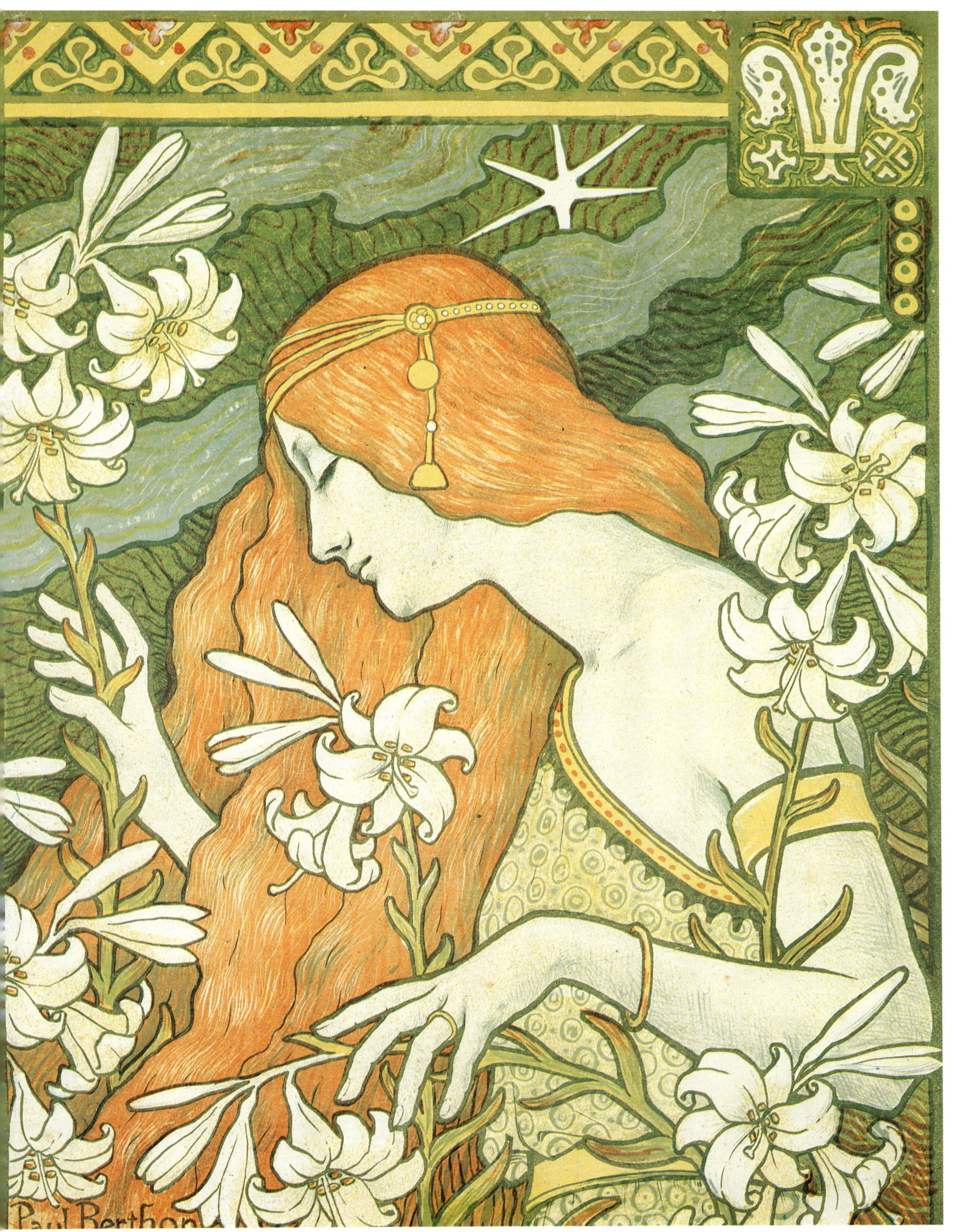
Paul Berthon

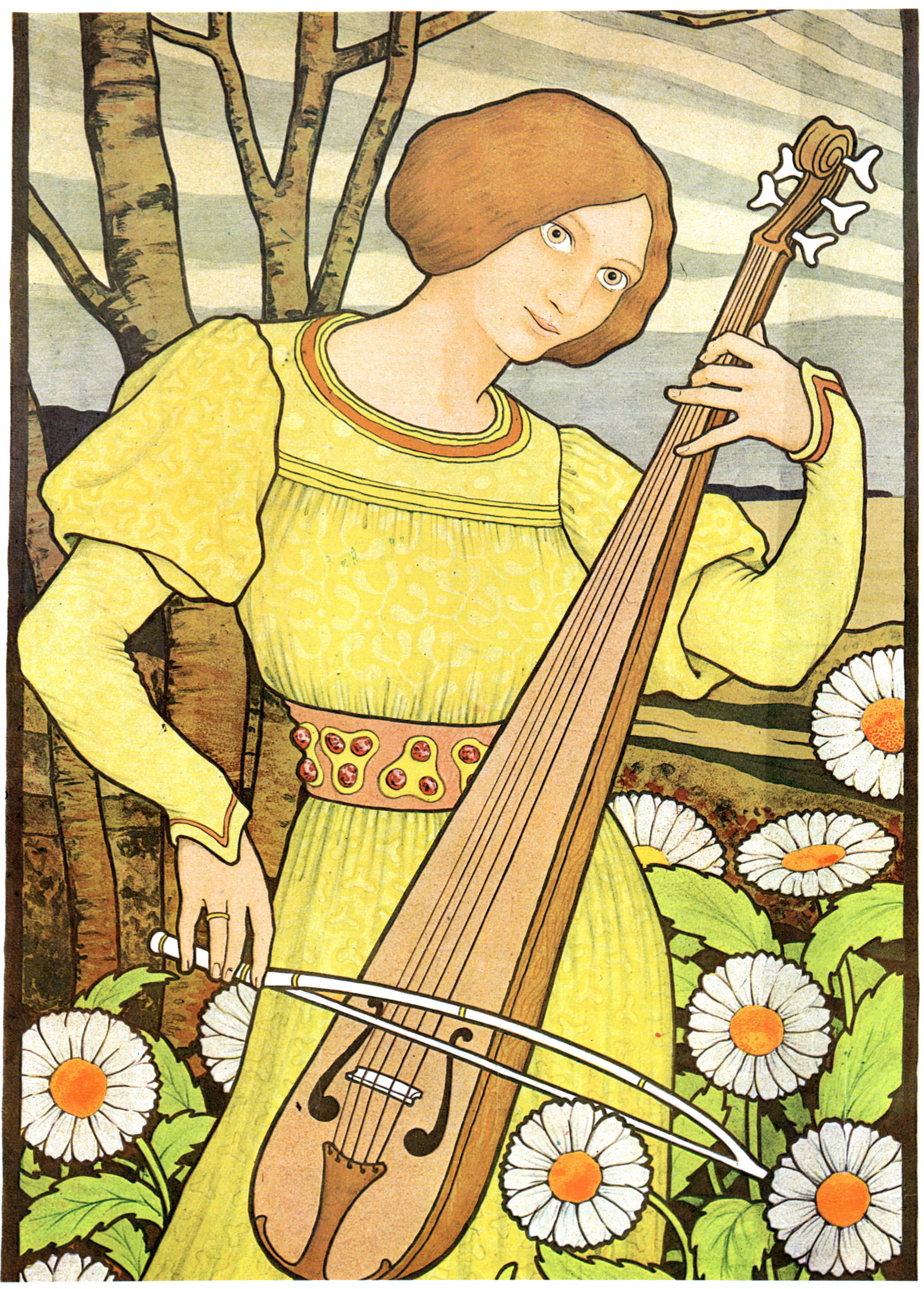

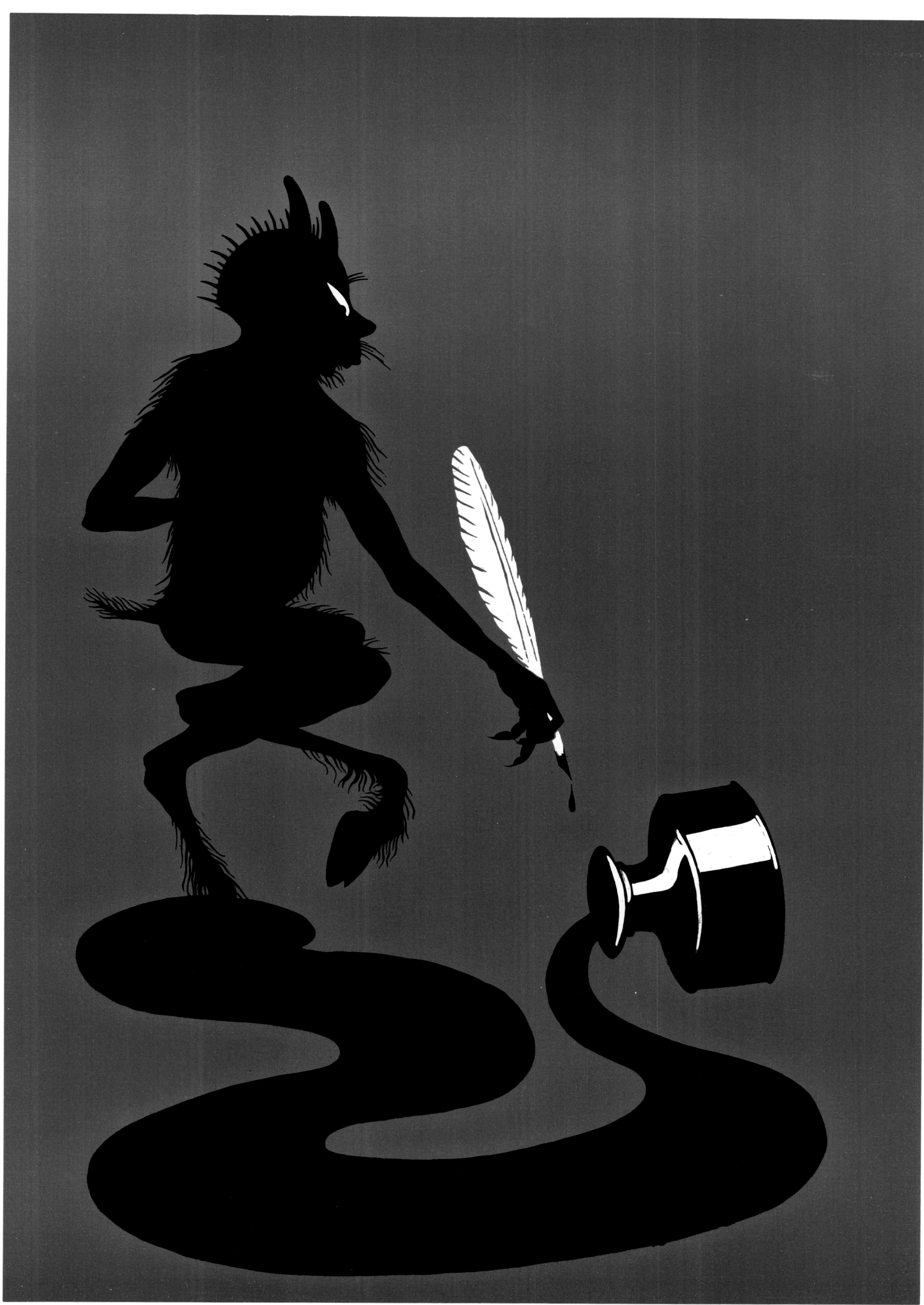

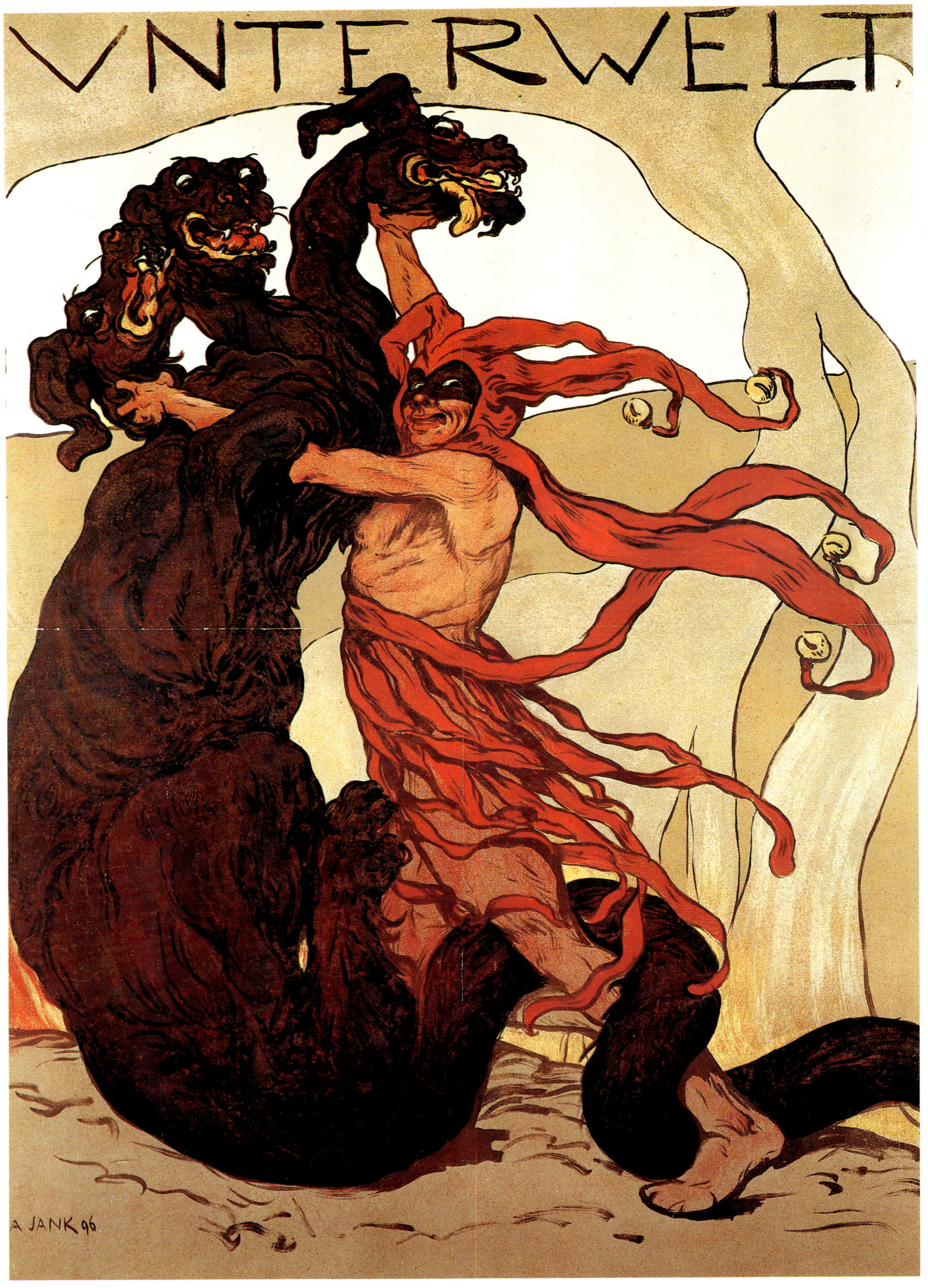
UNTERWELT
A JANK 96

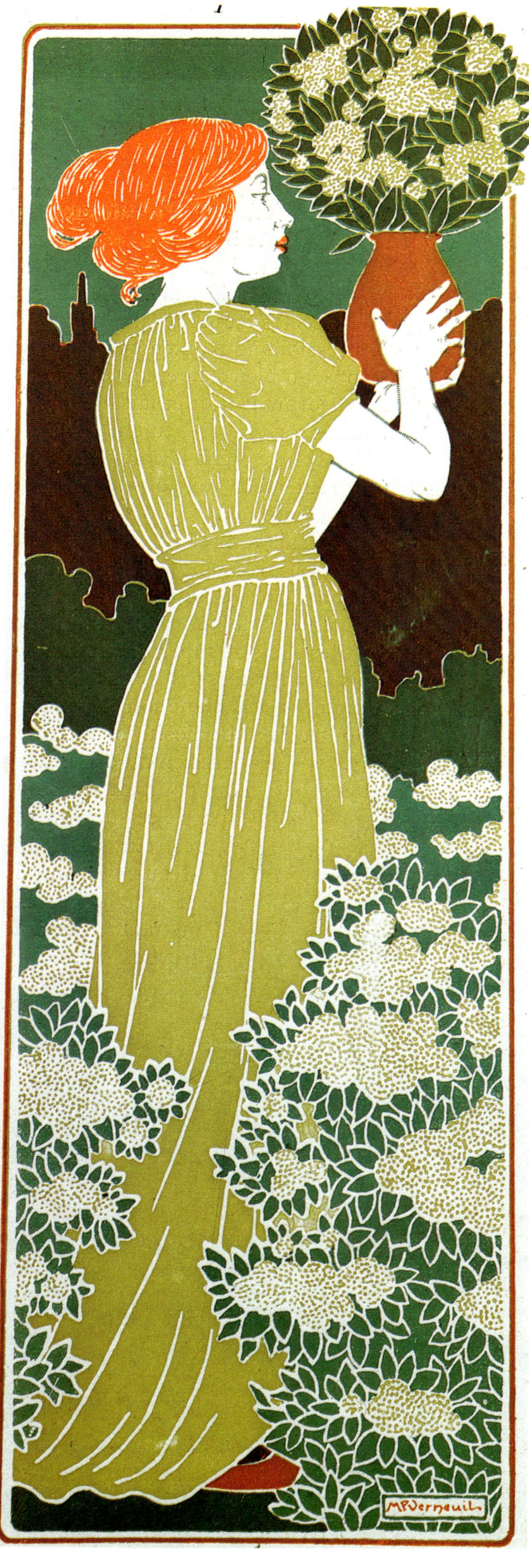
MPVerneuil

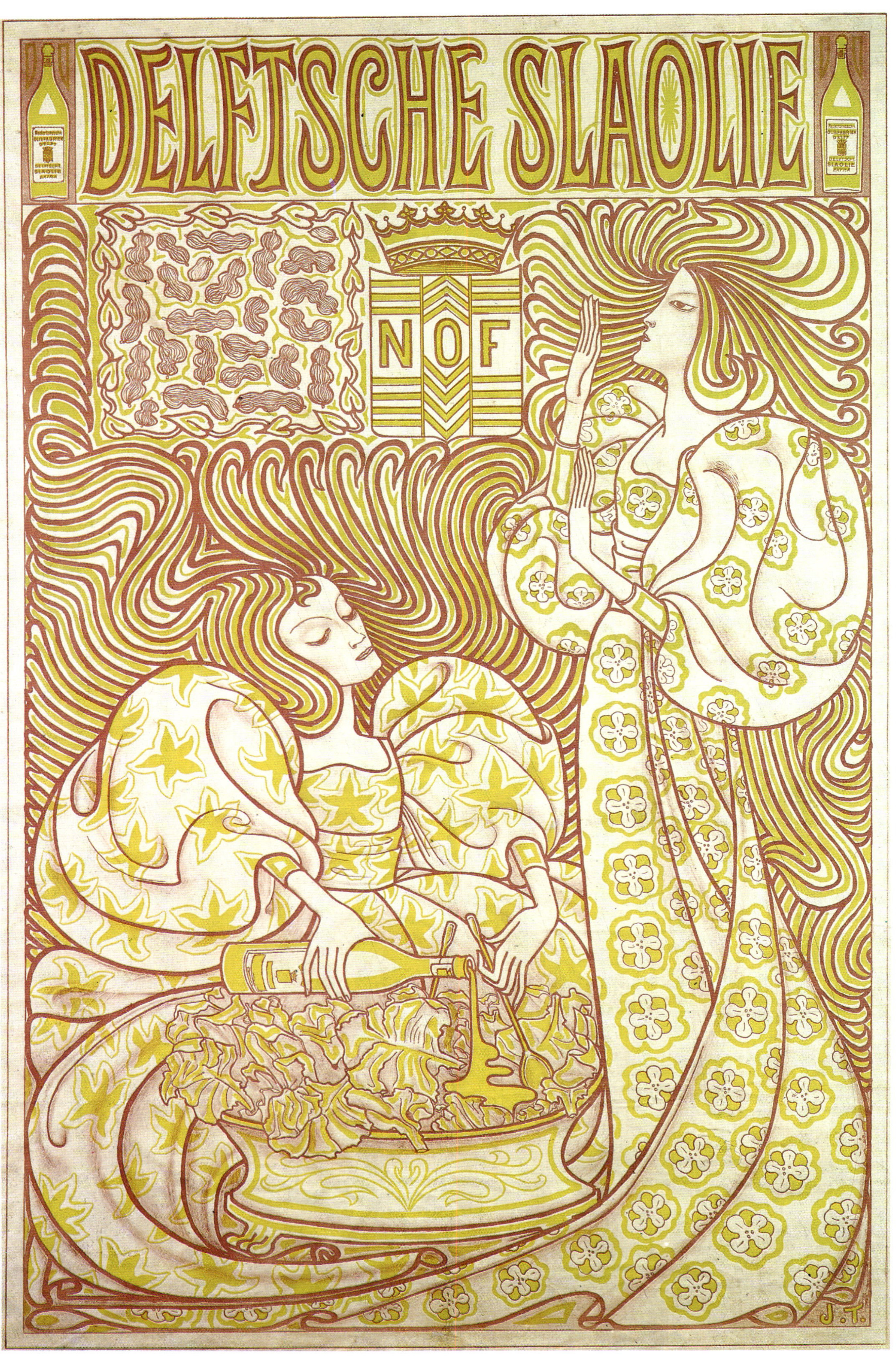
DELFTSCHE SLAOLIE
NOF
J.T.

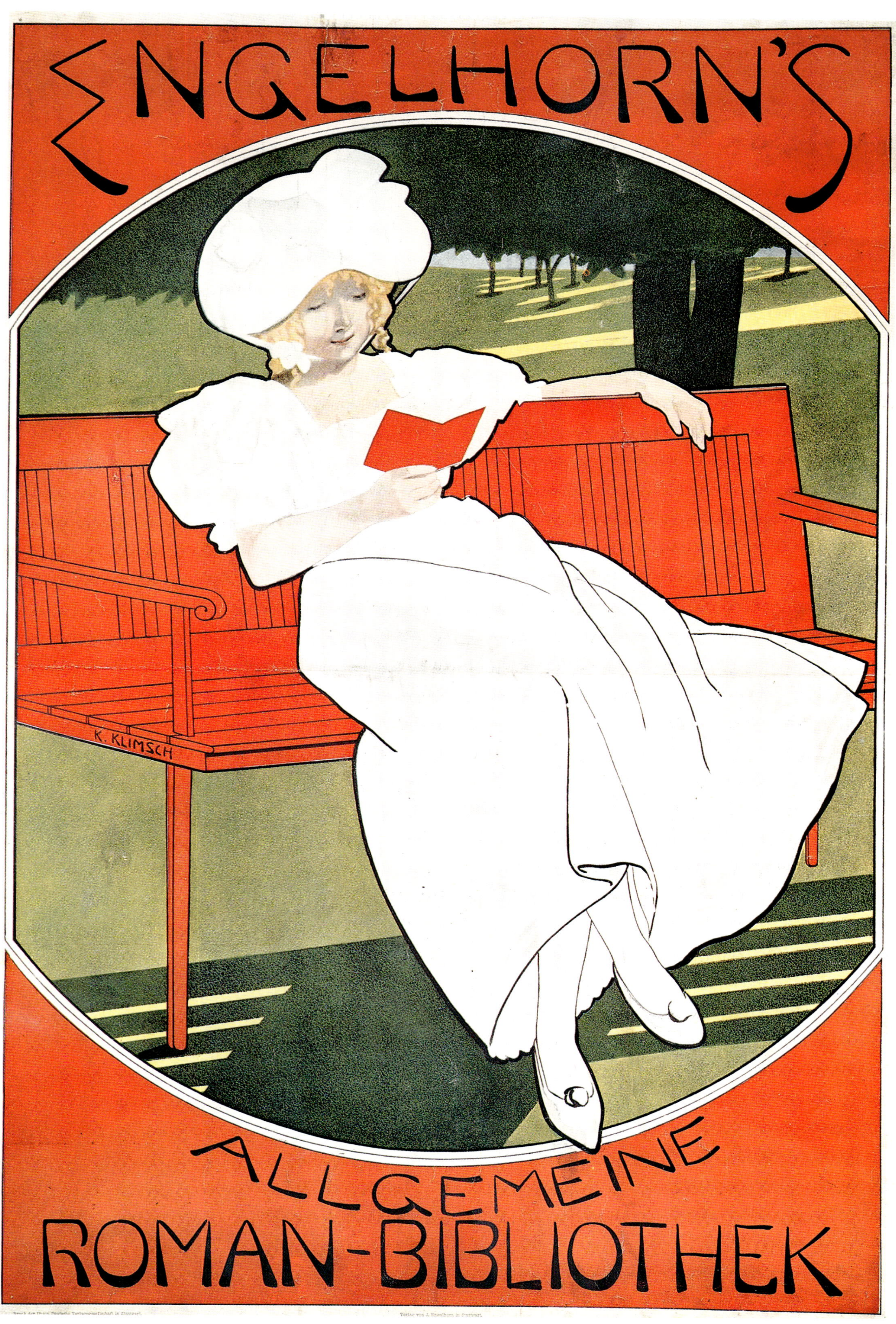
ENGELHORN'S
K. KLIMSCH
ALLGEMEINE
ROMAN-BIBLIOTHEK

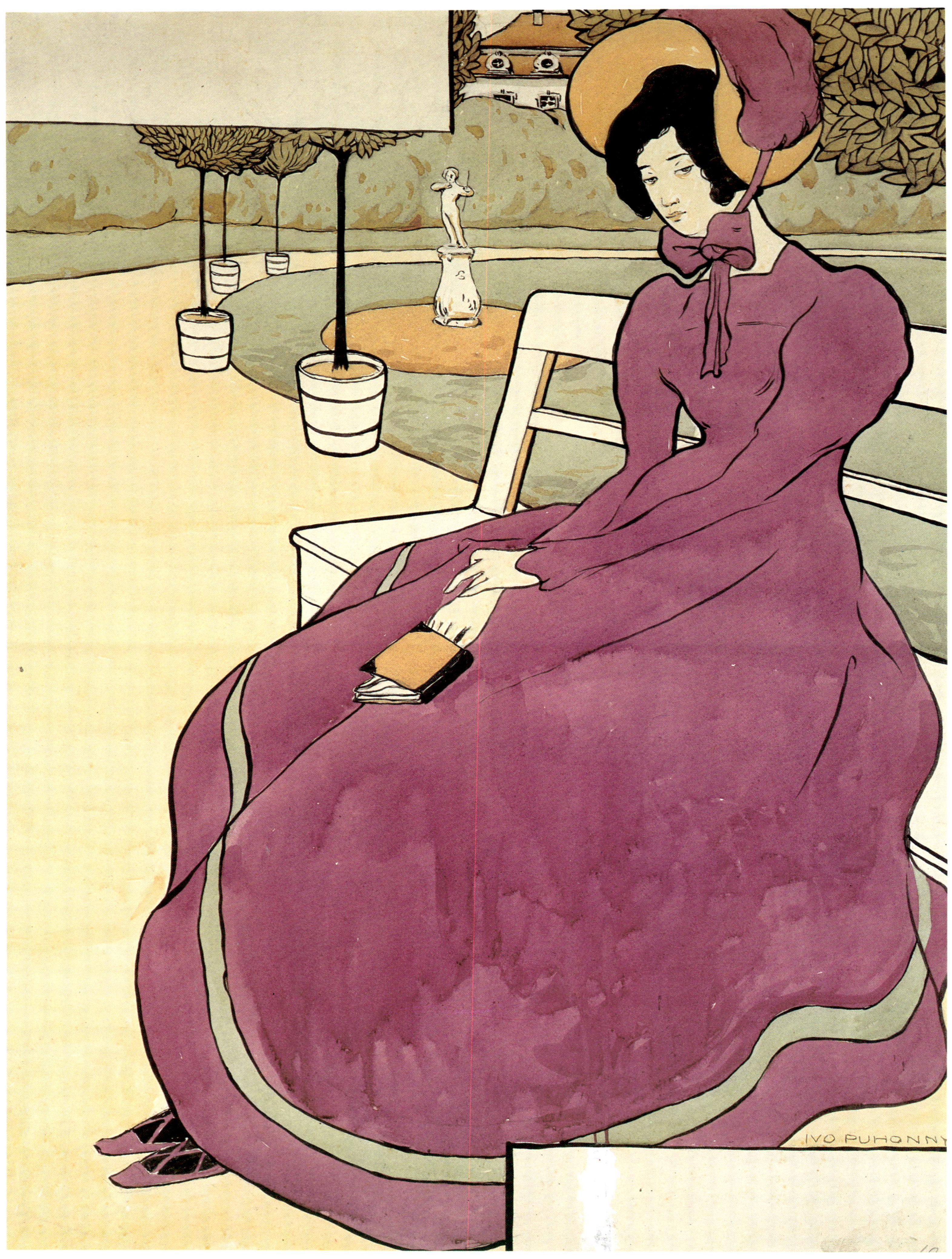
IVO PUHONNY

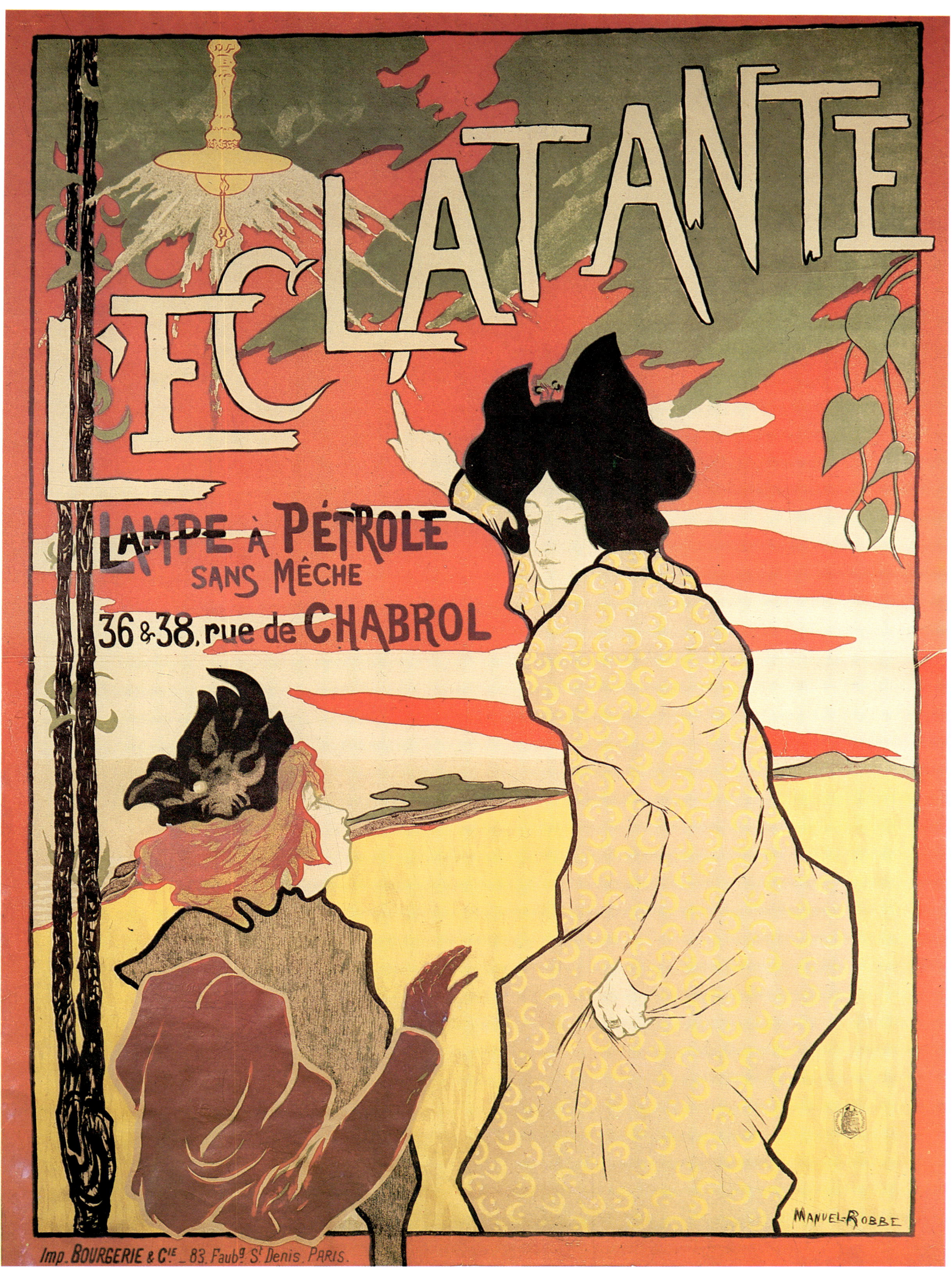
L'ECLATANTE
LAMPE À PÉTROLE
SANS MÈCHE
36 & 38, rue de CHABROL
MANUEL-ROBBE
Imp. BOURGERIE & Cie _ 83, Faubg St Denis, PARIS.

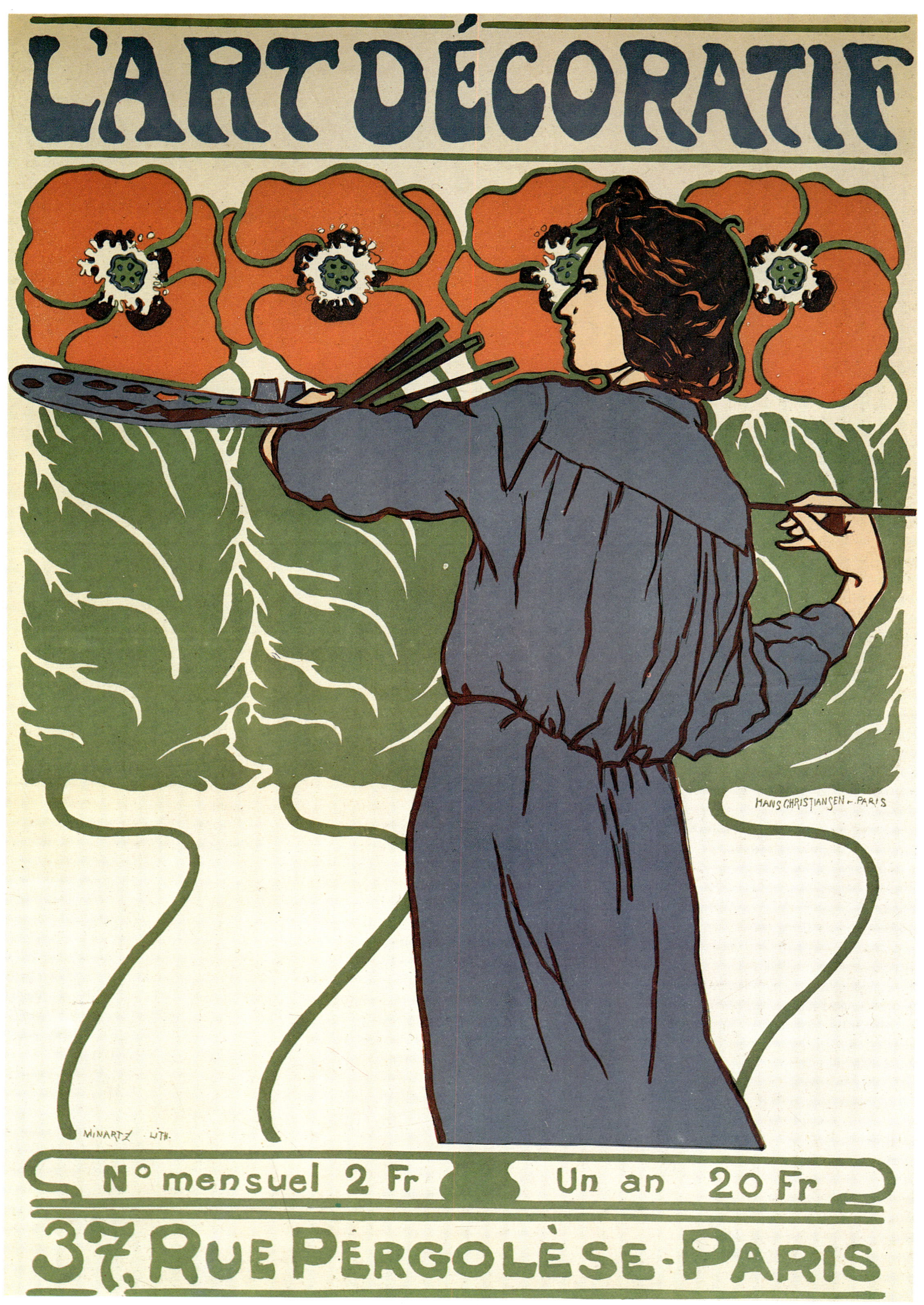
L'ART DÉCORATIF
HANS CHRISTIANSEN - PARIS
MINARTZ LITH.
N° mensuel 2 Fr
Un an 20 Fr
37, RUE PERGOLÈSE - PARIS

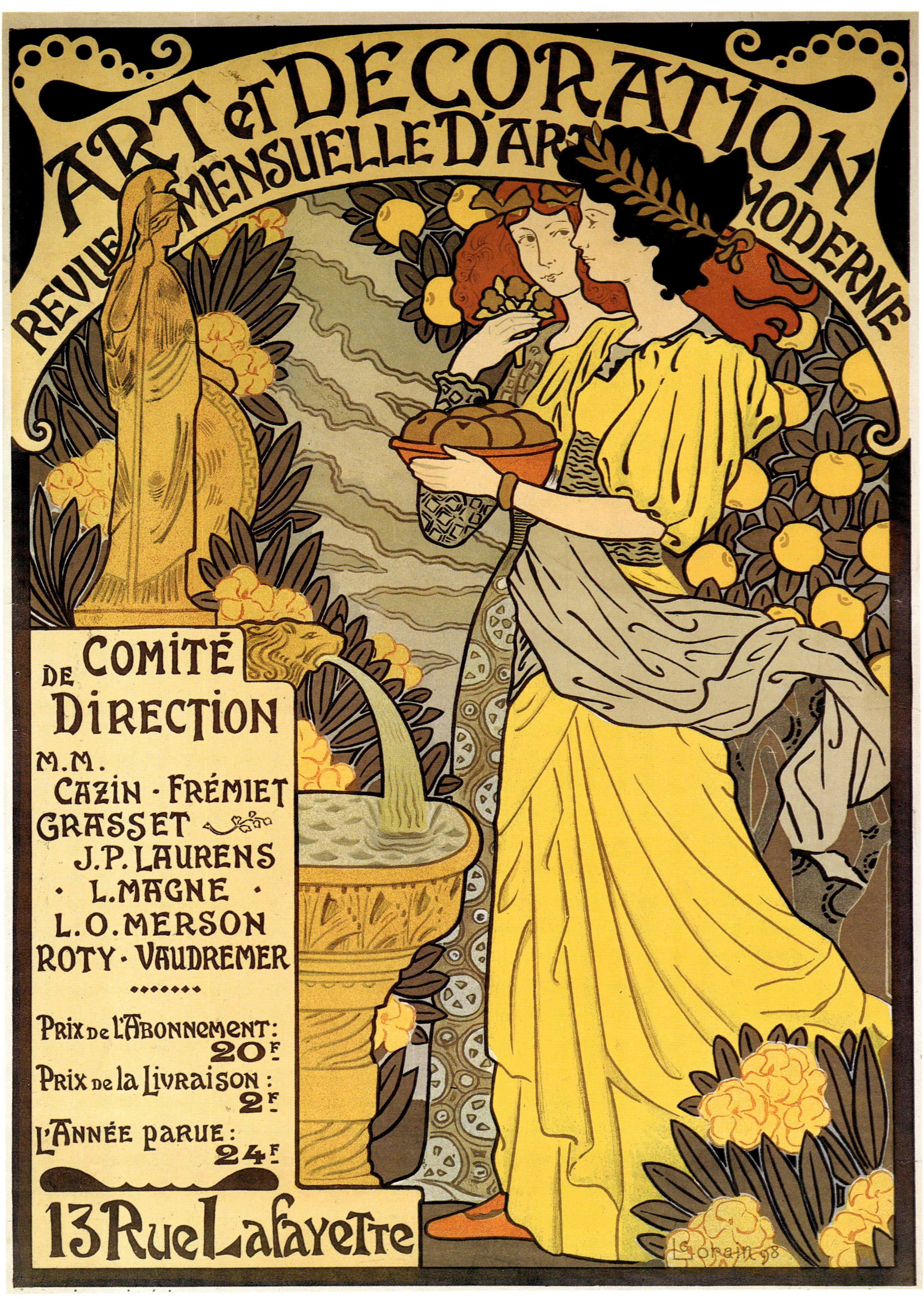
ART et DECORATION
REVUE MENSUELLE D'ART MODERNE
COMITÉ DE DIRECTION
M.M.
CAZIN · FRÉMIET
GRASSET
J.P. LAURENS
· L.MAGNE ·
L.O.MERSON
ROTY · VAUDREMER
Prix de l'Abonnement: 20F.
Prix de la Livraison: 2F.
L'Année parue: 24F.
13 Rue Lafayette
L. Gorain 98

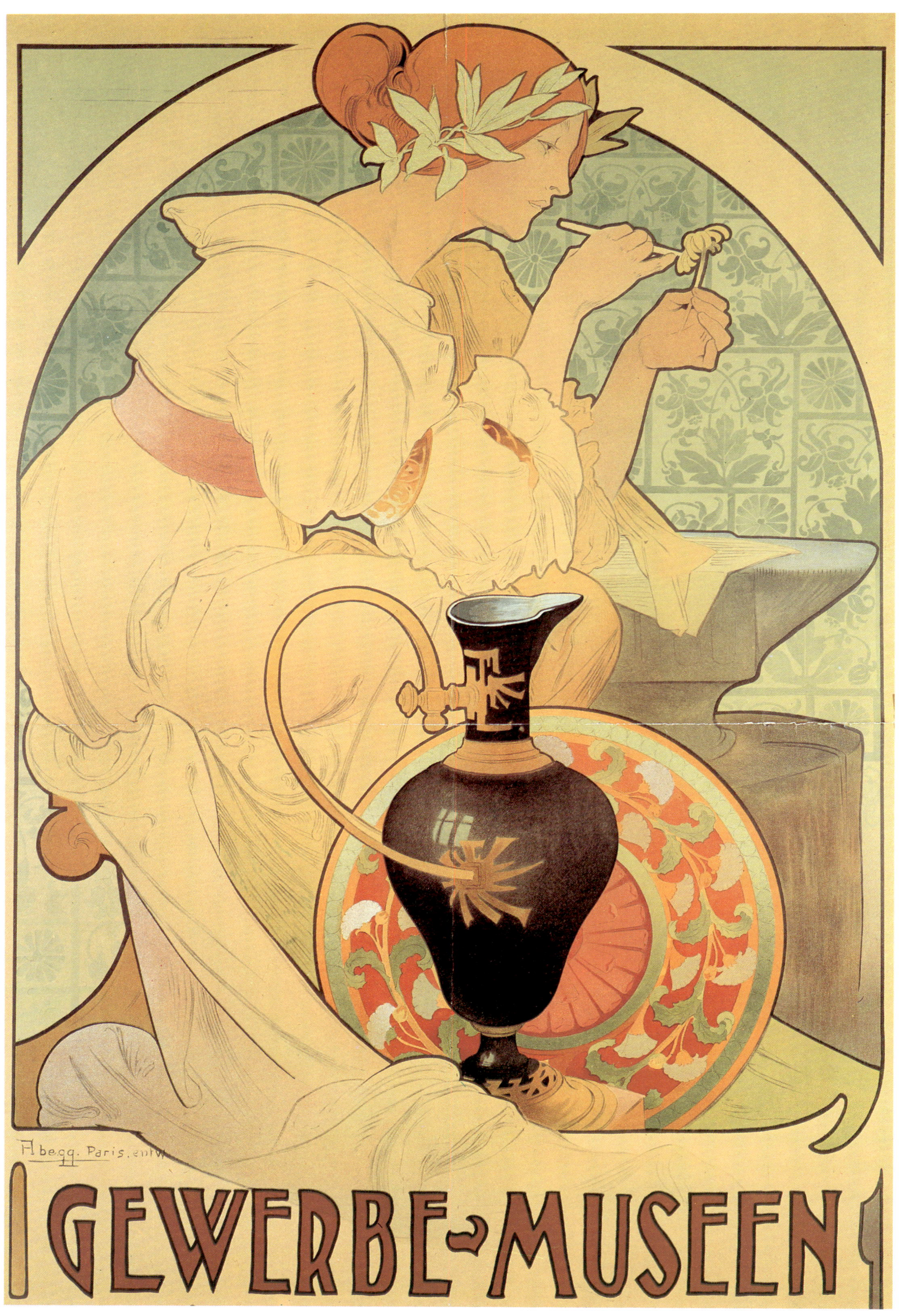
A. Abegg. Paris. entw.
GEWERBE-MUSEEN

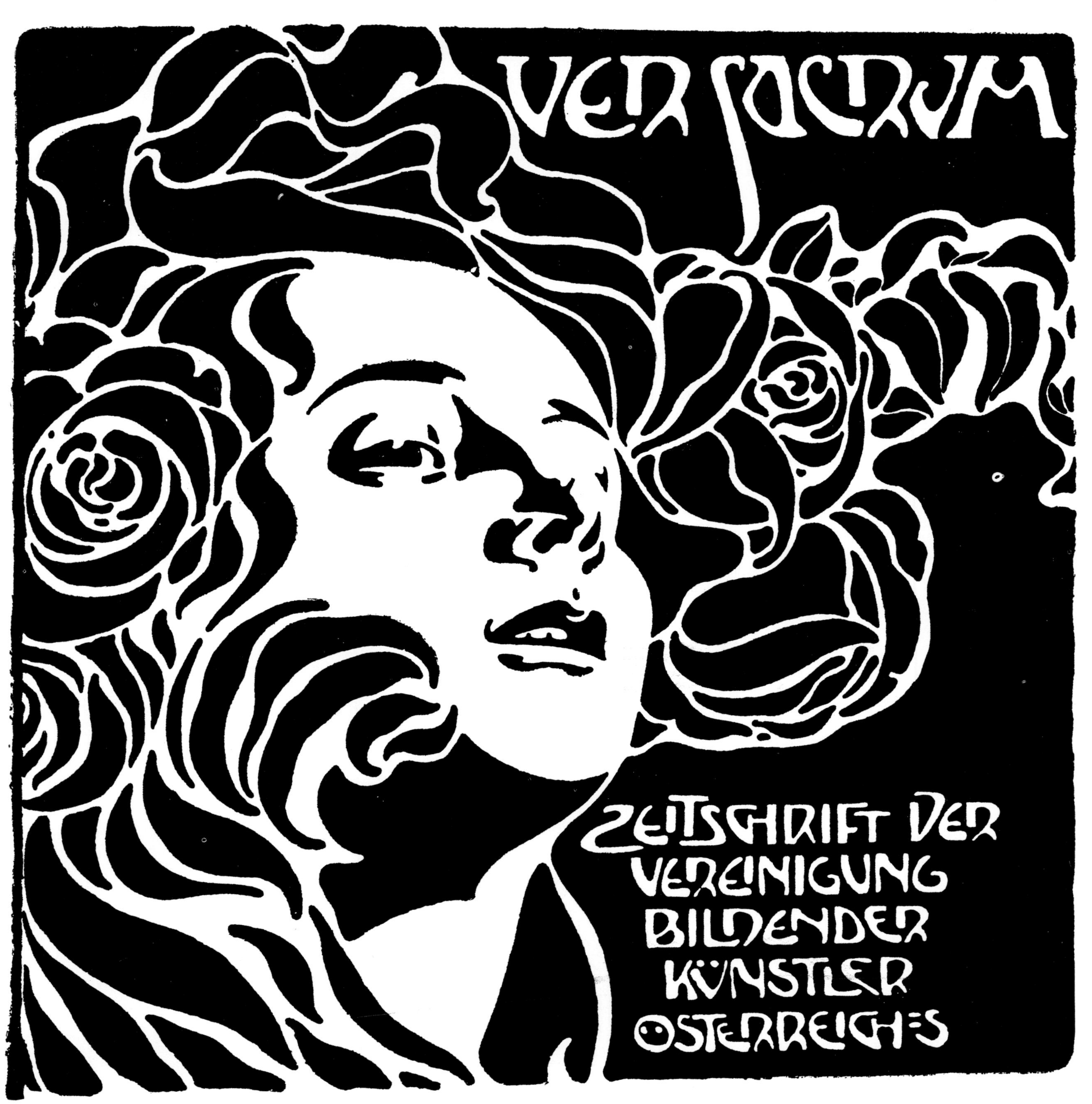
VER SACRUM
ZEITSCHRIFT DER
VEREINIGUNG
BILDENDER
KÜNSTLER
ÖSTERREICHES

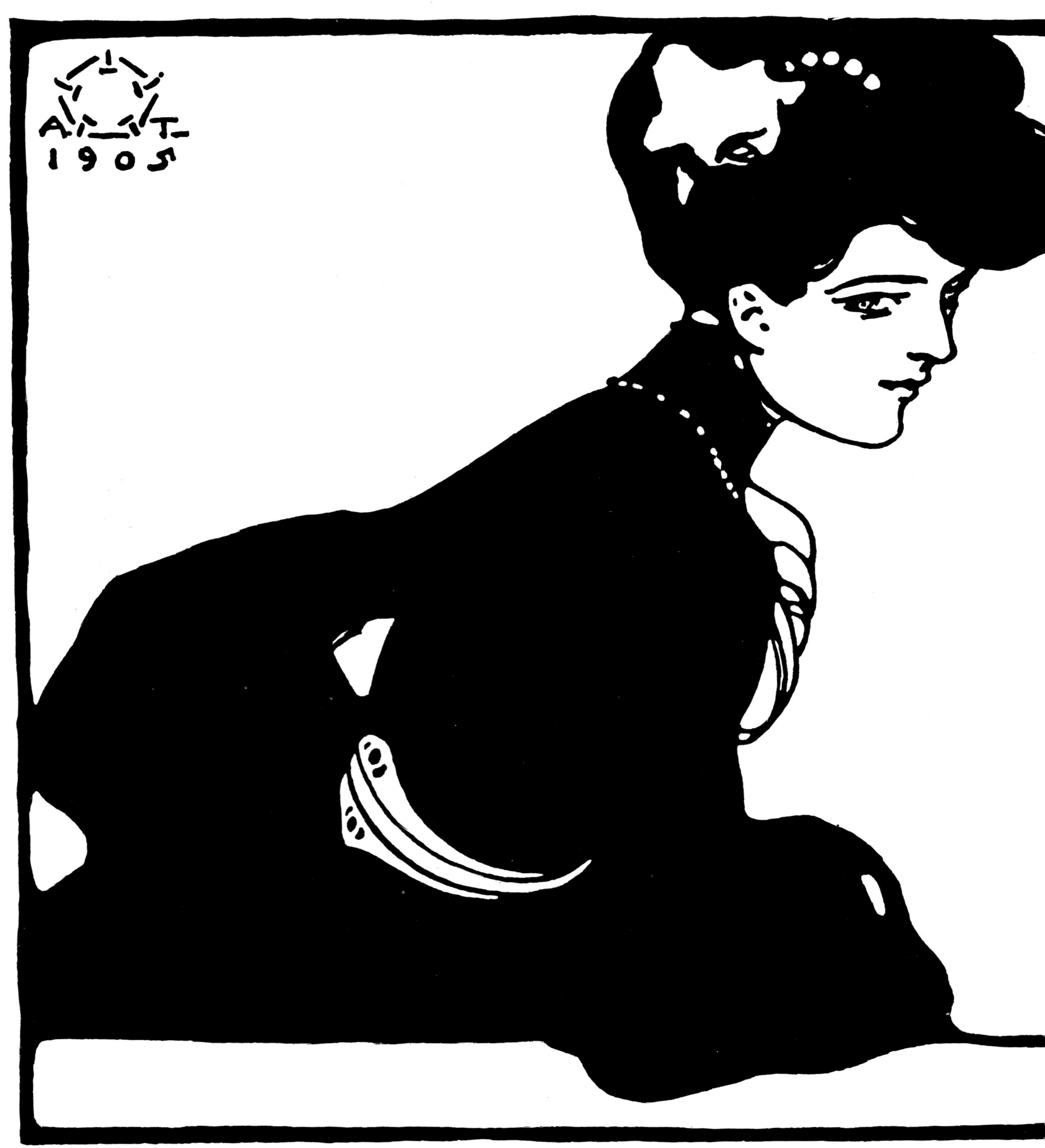
A T
1905

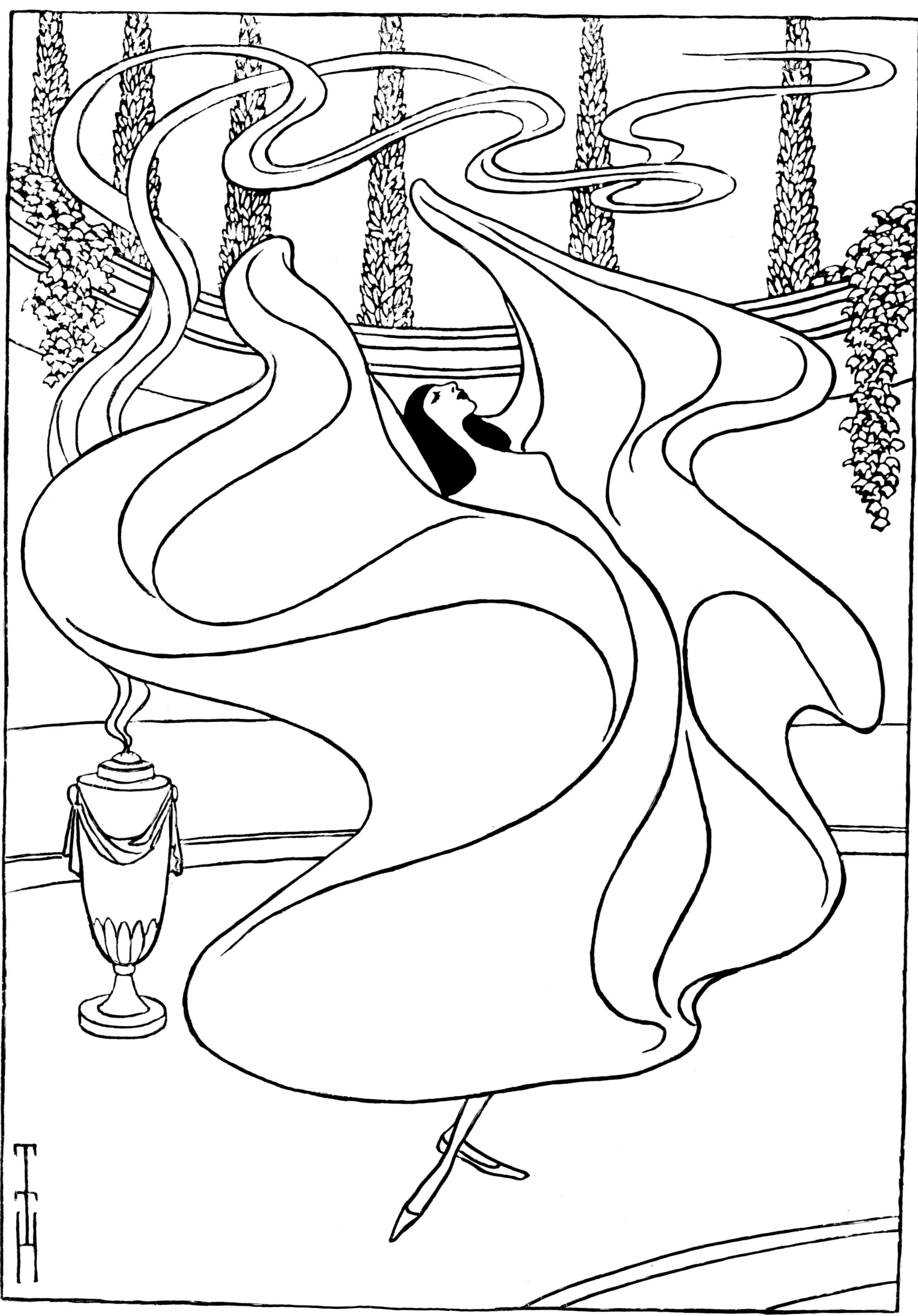

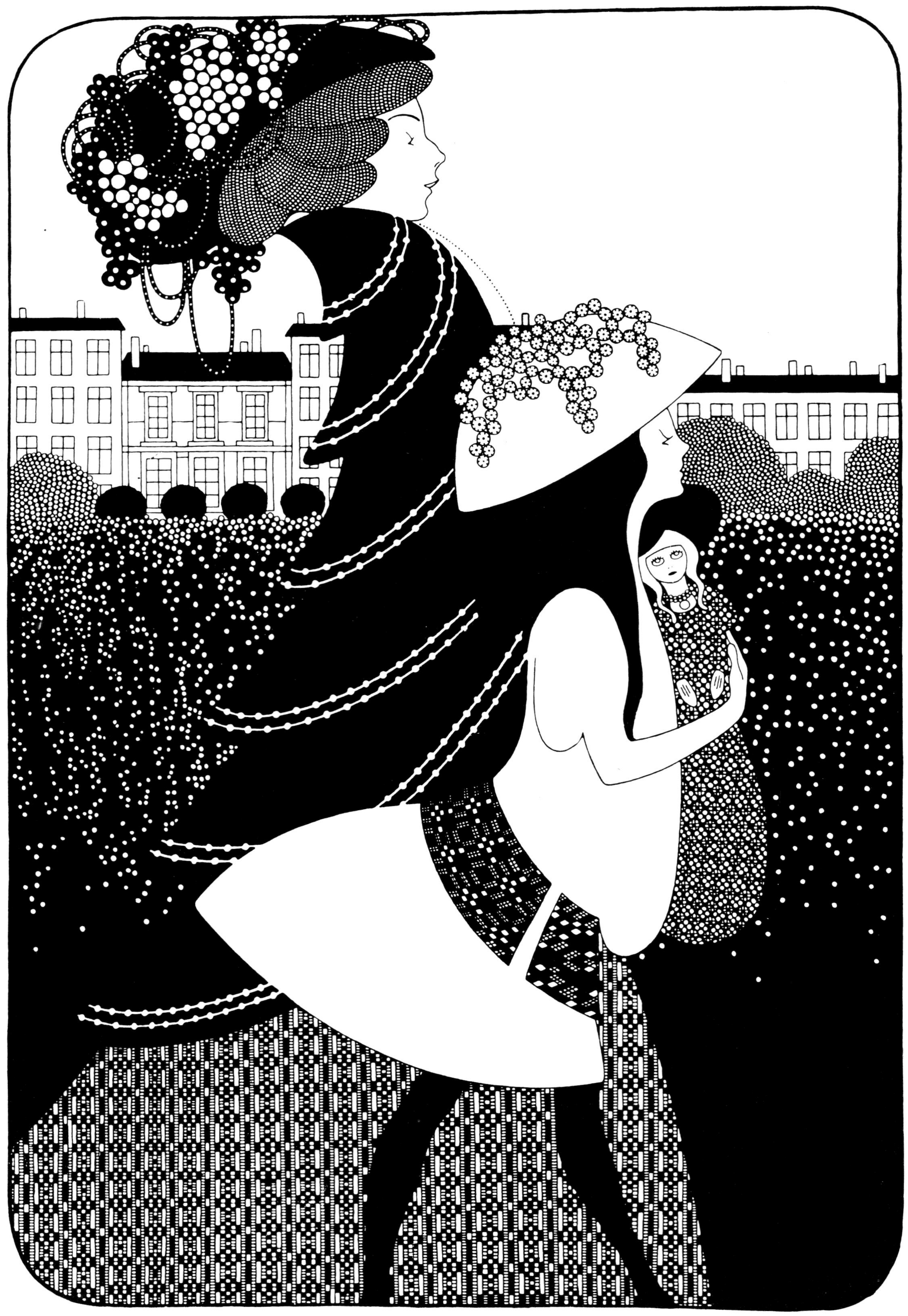

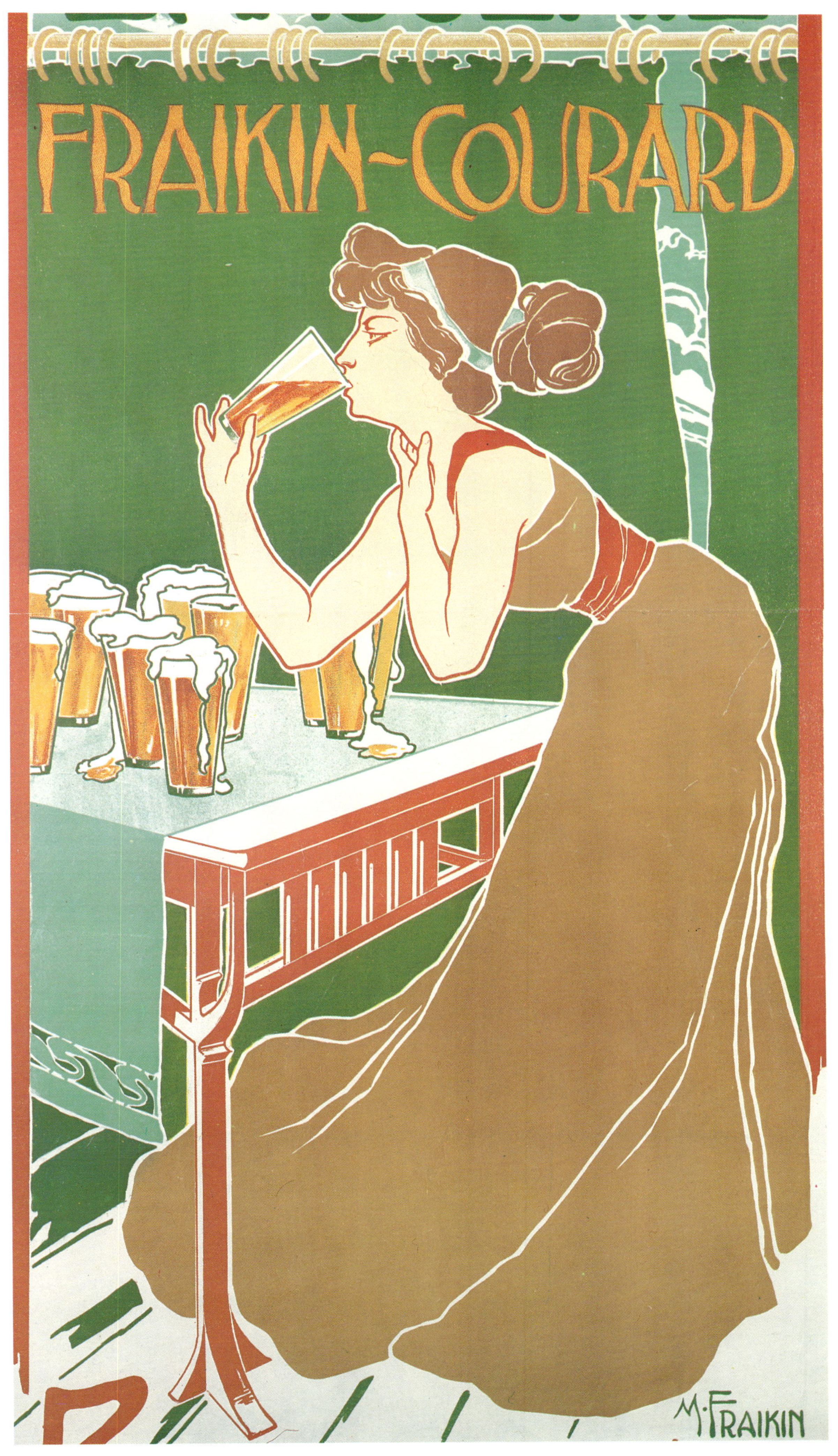
FRAIKIN-COURARD
M. FRAIKIN

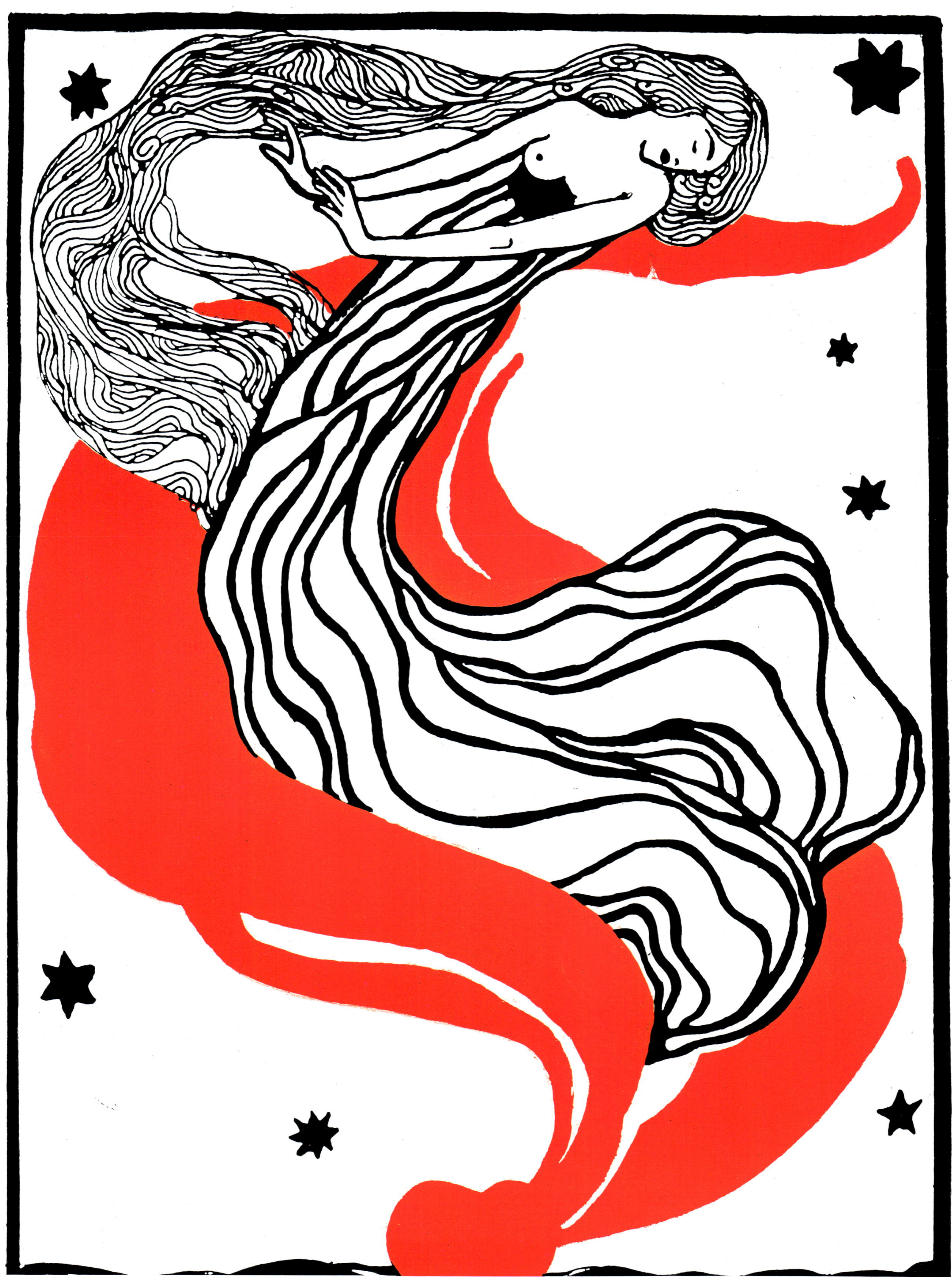

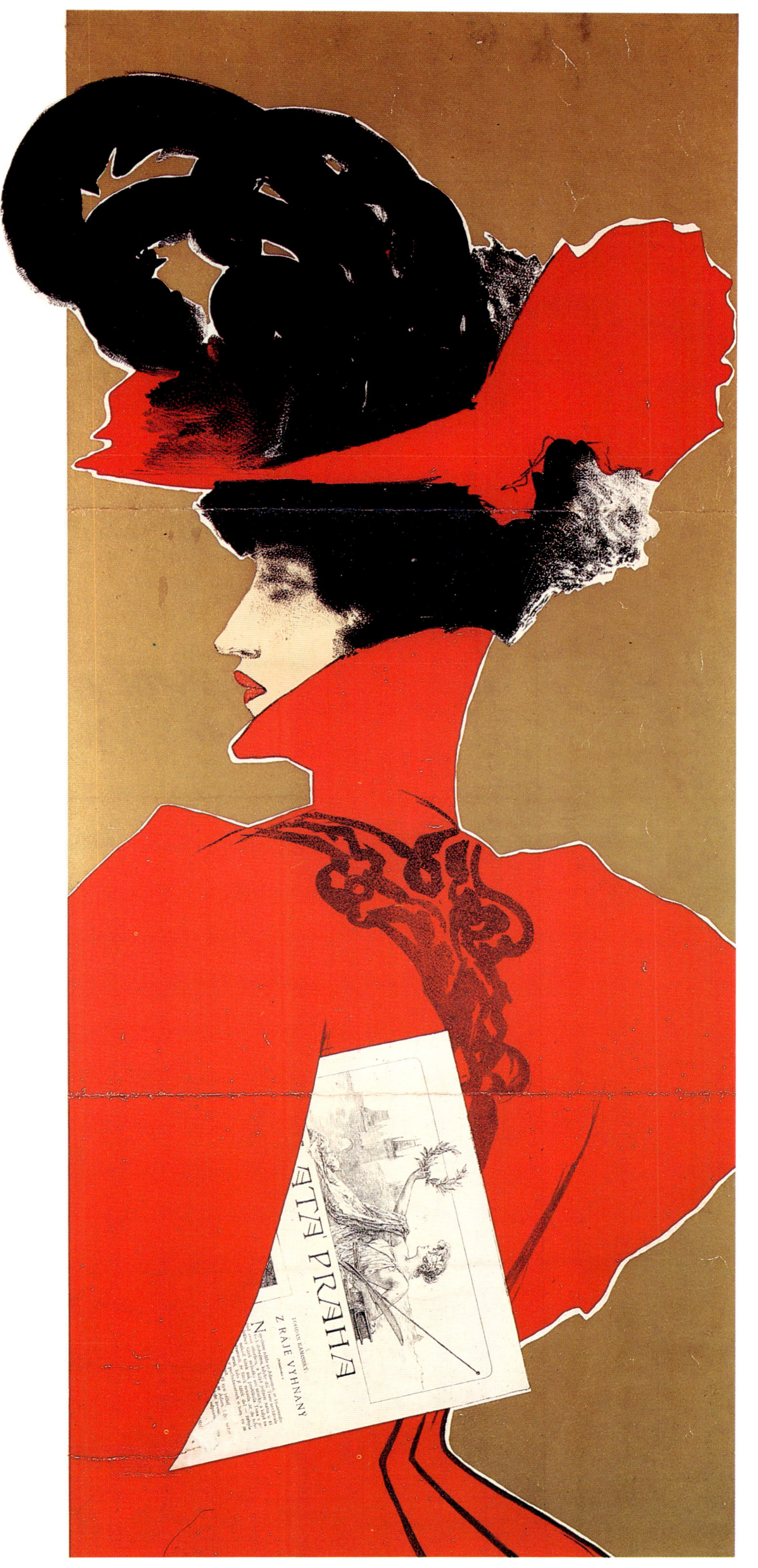
ATA PRAHA
Z RÁJE VYHNANÝ

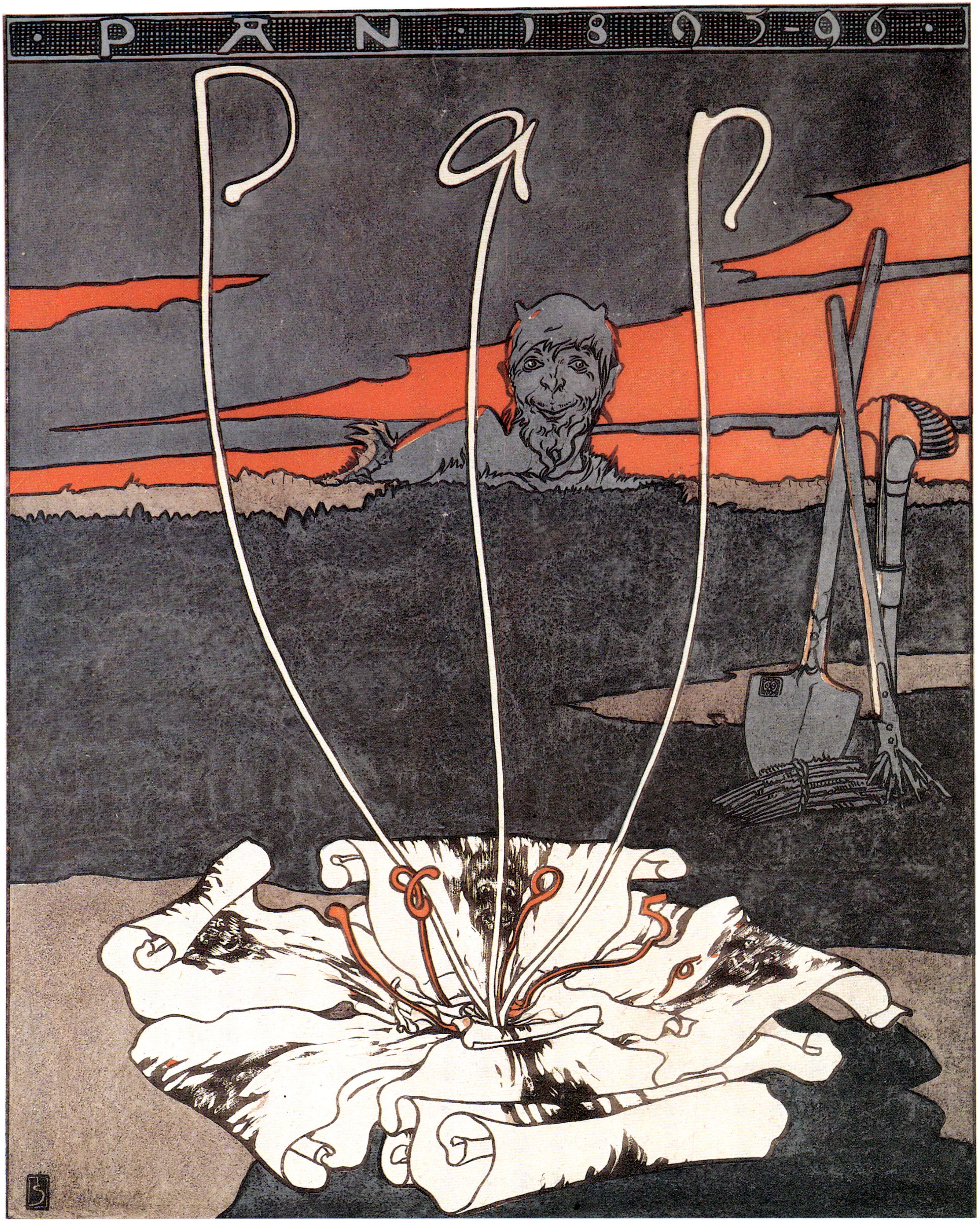
PAN · 1895-96
Pan

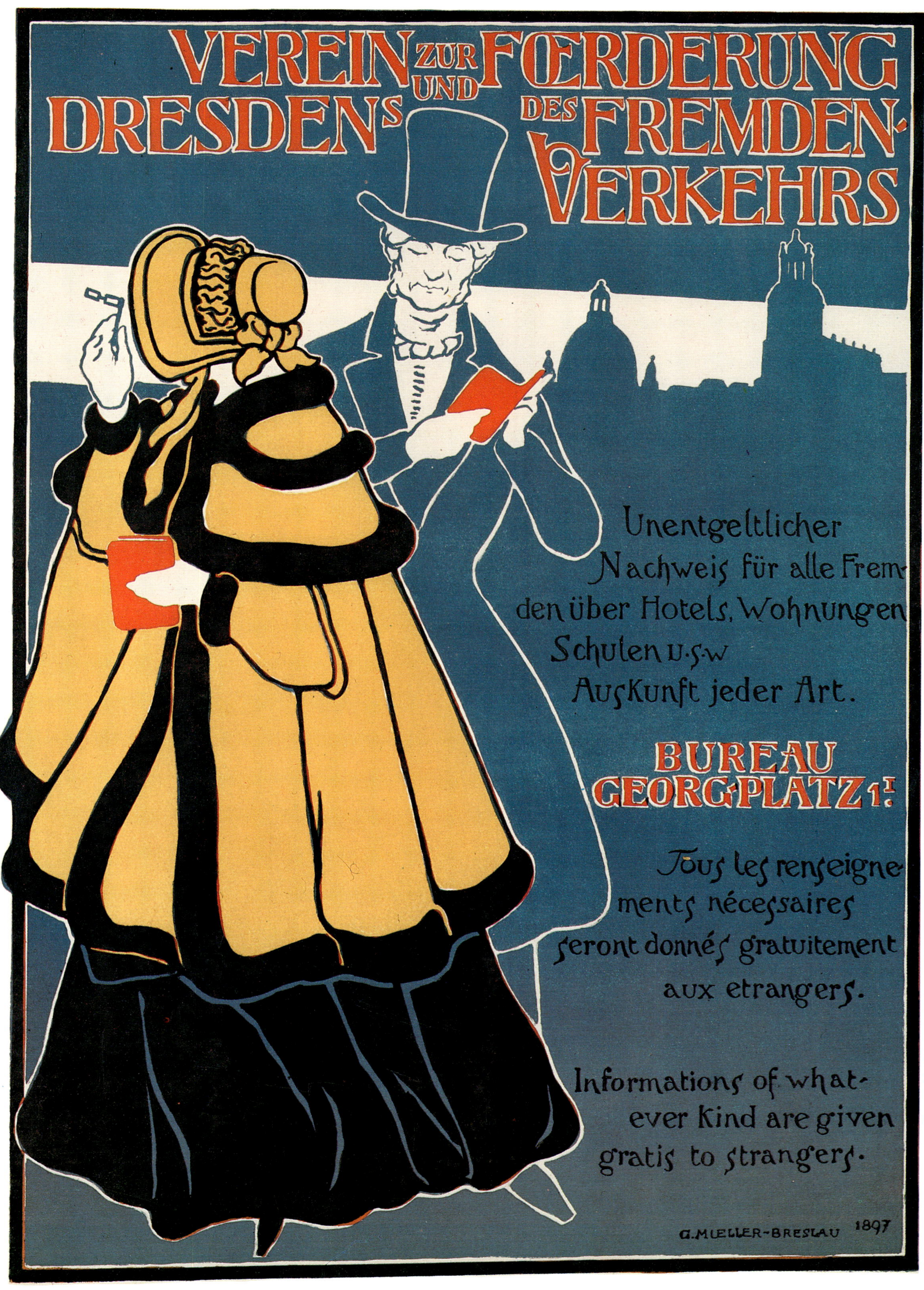
VEREIN ZUR FOERDERUNG
DRESDENS UND DES FREMDEN-
VERKEHRS
Unentgeltlicher
Nachweis für alle Frem-
den über Hotels, Wohnungen
Schulen u.s.w
Auskunft jeder Art.
BUREAU
GEORG-PLATZ 1.I
Tous les renseigne-
ments nécessaires
seront donnés gratuitement
aux etrangers.
Informations of what-
ever kind are given
gratis to strangers.
G. MUELLER-BRESLAU 1897

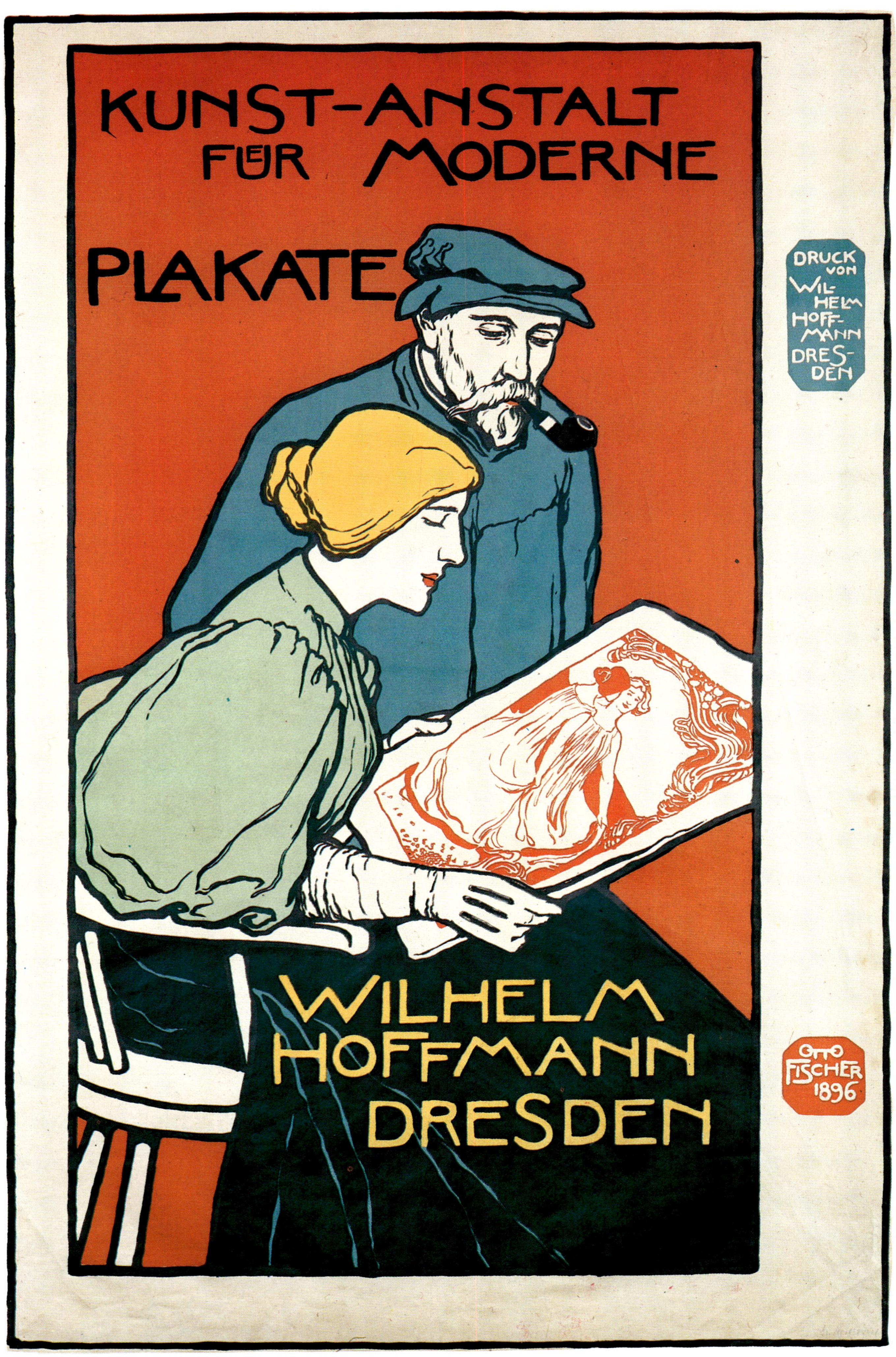
KUNST-ANSTALT
FÜR MODERNE
PLAKATE
DRUCK VON WILHELM HOFFMANN DRESDEN
WILHELM
HOFFMANN
DRESDEN
OTTO FISCHER 1896

# TABLE OF ILLUSTRATIONS